TIMMINS

THE PORCUPINE COUNTRY

- Timmins Museum

TIMMINS

THE PORCUPINE COUNTRY

Michael Barnes

An early view of the McIntyre Mine.   - OA 3068-18

THE BOSTON MILLS PRESS

This book is dedicated to
my wife
Joan Wyatt Barnes
who has made it possible for me to become a writer.

ISBN 1-55046-050-1

© Michael Barnes, 1991

Published by:
THE BOSTON MILLS PRESS
132 Main Street
Erin, Ontario N0B 1T0
(519) 833-2407
Fax: (519) 833-2195

Cover Design by Gillian Stead
Book Design by Carolyn Klymko
Edited by Noel Hudson
Typography by Lexigraf, Tottenham
Printed by Ampersand, Guelph

The publisher wishes to acknowledge the financial assistance and
encouragement of The Canada Council, the Ontario Arts Council and
the Office of the Secretary of State.

Pearl Lake.

Pearl Lake was an early favourite for Sunday outings.   - OA 3068-117

Contents

Workers on Mattagami Road were hard to keep for mine wages were much better.

- OA 3637-21

Acknowledgements

People who stand out among those who, by their enthusiasm and kindness, helped to make this book possible are Don Thompson, Secretary to the Mine Managers, Roberta Carey and Helen Bilodeau of the Chamber of Commerce, and Jack Watson, Clerk of the City of Timmins.

The assistance of the Timmins Economic Development Corporation is appreciated.

City contributors were Mayor Denis Welin and his secretary, Lorraine Demers; Judy Cassidy and the Public Library staff (I share their hope for a new building); Karen Guillemette of the Convention Bureau; Karen Bachman and the Museum staff; Chief Dennis Harris and Jim Thompson, Ernie Fischofer and Randy Stojkiewicz of the Timmins Police; Bert Schaffer, Fire Chief; Carol Johannsen of Golden Manor; and Kees Pols of the Mattagami Conservation Authority.

Mining assistance was provided by Doug McNair of the Mining Corporation; Charles Gryba, Moneta; Mark Mitchell, Barry Hope and Jim Lanay of Pamour; Chris Hamblin, Core Library; Andy Mallinson of Kidd; and Cliff McFadden, assayer.

Business sector helpers were Mert Lake of the *Porcupine Advance*; Bill Boychuk and Larry Brooksbank, Hydro; Jim Thompson Sr., Henry Ostrosser and George Scott of Northern Allied Supply; Yvon Jodouin of Underground Treasures; and Christof Weidner of Christof's Jewellery.

Lumber industry background was provided by Nicole Malette of Malette Inc. and George Barron of McChesney Lumber.

Media aid was provided by Richard Buell of the *Daily Press* and Michael Doody of Mid-Canada Television.

Other support came from Jean Lanthier, La Ronde; Dr. A. Hukowich, Medical Officer of Health; Nancy Perger, Ukrainian Museum; Rt. Rev. Caleb Lawrence, Bishop of Moosonee; Dennis Austin and staff at the Ojibway-Cree Centre; Margaret Haines, Jeanne Larcher, Joe Ferrari, Rene St. Pierre and George White.

People who kindly loaned old photographs are acknowledged in individual photo credits.

The colour photographs of Graeme Oxby grace the dust jacket of this book. People who processed photographs and otherwise assisted were Bill Forder, Peter Cliff, John Kirwan and Bob Atkinson.

As ever, Joyce Allick and Bryce Ross at Teck Centennial Library in Kirkland Lake provided their usual first-class service.

Peter DelGuidice kindly read the manuscript and made some suggestions for its improvement.

'Princess' Maggie, seen skinning a beaver, claimed to be descended from a survivor of the Frederick House massacre.
- Bill Boychuk collection

Introduction

The City of Timmins is the centre of the Porcupine country of Northern Ontario, an amalgamation of the former communities of Mountjoy, Schumacher, Timmins, South Porcupine and Porcupine. For a municipality that is home to less than 50,000 people, Timmins holds in its 1,239 square miles the distinction of being the largest city in Canada in terms of land area.

In common with Sudbury, its nearest neighbour city, 185 miles to the southeast, Timmins owes its existence to the mining industry. But both cities have seen economic diversification in recent years, a move welcomed by residents, as a variety of employment sources eases the roller-coaster boom-and-bust ride often experienced by single-industry communities.

As Timmins assumes the role of regional centre, it cannot shake association with its resource-based past. The city's single largest employer is still a mining company, and the next largest is the forest industry. Saw log and pulpwood trucks are common sights on area highways. Headframes stand out on the horizon. Some are inactive, mute reminders of their working past, while others still take men and machinery underground so that precious and base metals may be brought to the surface.

Mining towns were once known as camps. The idea was that such places would not last. They were spots to camp until the ore ran out and temporary residents went home. Yet "camps" such as Cobalt, Kirkland Lake, Sudbury and Timmins have confounded the pessimists and refused to become ghost towns. Somehow the hard-working, adventuresome spirit of their citizens has never been mined out.

Porcupine residents never forget that this place was founded on dreams. The chance of finding the pot of gold at the end of the trail kept prospectors going. In many cases the only legacy of this quest remains in a name. The Reef Mine suggested gold-bearing quartz. Nabob implied a wealthy person, the investor. The presence of precious metal was intimated in names like Aunor and Goldhawk, while Crown and Paymaster tempted with the suggestion of later reward. The Moneta Mine was a direct promise, moneta being the Italian word for coin. Where chances of discovery were based more on faith than reason, the name Hope appears, while others dignified themselves as a Prospect.

Optimism, after all, is a necessary part of the prospector's rig. Many of those single-minded individuals who hit the trail with a packsack, pick, shovel and a hunch contributed to the growth of a great city. A few are honoured in Timmins' street names – Bannerman, Davidson, Gillies, Hollinger, McIntyre, Middleton, Preston, Vipond and Wilson. Men like these should not be forgotten, for they opened up a large part of the North Country.

A bush road winds away from the former Preston East Dome Mine to a long-forgotten mine site. The road crosses a flat expanse of sandy grit mine tailings and soon becomes overgrown in a tangle of bushes and tag alders. The visitor who continues up the road is presented with several tracks that fan out through the bush. The houses that once fronted these paths are gone now and only their basements remain. Many are marked by the remains of overgrown flower gardens, and large roses abound in the summer months. At the end of one road are the ruins of the New York Porcupine Mine. The small headframe is long gone and the shaft is capped. The nearby heavy concrete forms once supported the compressor and the hoist room.

This small mine was one of many which failed to produce a substantial deposit of gold. Its only producing year was 1933, when from 2,800 tons of ore a harvest of 153 ounces of gold realized a total of $5,202 as a return on a considerable investment. The name New York was no doubt coined to attract American investors. All who held on to their shares lost money. For these unfortunate people and their families, the only tangible souvenir of the venture exists today in elegant but worthless stock certificates.

The Porcupine district survived numerous mine closings as well as forest fires,, floods, strikes and depressed times. The Timmins-Porcupine story is one of determined people who came to the wild bush country and made it their home.

The old picture hardly does justice to the contrast between milky quartz and the host rock. An outcrop like this started the gold rush.

- OA S13738

Prologue to the Porcupine

Over a billion years ago the Canadian Shield country went through great geological change. As the earth's permanent crust formed, rocks were twisted, folded, detached and piled into great mountains. Volcanoes erupted, fissures appeared in the rock, and molten material from deep in the earth's interior swept up through these intrusions to the surface. The newer rock cooled and became part of the land, but in some places it carried a treasure trove of minerals. Gold, silver, copper, lead, zinc and nickel awaited discovery.

The ancient folded rock which predominates in the Porcupine is known as the Greenstone Belt and it is coupled with sediments. A 2-mile-wide stretch runs east to west across the townships of Tisdale and Whitney for 12 miles. The Hollinger and McIntyre mines stake out the north end and the Dome Mine lies to the south. This area was one which received an extraordinarily large share of both precious and base metals. The mountains wore down over millions of years, but much of the minerals remained.

During the last million years great sheets of ice ebbed and flowed in a north-south path across the land. The age of ice totally changed the surface of the continent. A tilt in the earth's axis sent masses of Arctic ice into Canada and the northern United States. Existing hills and mountains were crushed and altered as the sheer weight of ice shaped and polished the land. Much evidence remains today of four such great ice movements, the last of which receded only 10,000 years ago.

Timmins is near the edge of what was once a huge glacial lake which stretched from the modern town of Kapuskasing east into Quebec. The 200-mile-long stretch of soil left from its bed is known as the Great Clay Belt. A similar, smaller belt runs from Englehart to New Liskeard. Hollows left behind when the great ice sheets finally receded became the beds of thousands of lakes. Scoured rocks clearly indicate the paths taken by the glaciers. Bulldozers at work on highway projects routinely uncover pebbles in clay and gravel which tend to point in the same direction, that of the ice mass which deposited them. Single boulders found in the bush are part of the debris left by receding ice, while eskers, long ridges of sand and gravel, were left behind by streams which flowed beneath the ice sheets. The City of Timmins sits on one such esker.

The sands, gravel and clay of Southern Ontario were all scraped from land to the north. Light-coloured crystalline granitic rock and sediments were left in the North. Often the gold held in the ancient northern rock was so fine as not to be visible to the naked eye, but in some cases visible gold appeared in veins where the ice had bared the host rock. Gradually this bonanza was covered with moss and forest humus. There it remained until men literally stumbled upon the precious mineral which had been hidden for thousands of years.

The land that held the gold was thickly wooded country. This boreal forest mainly held conifers, with occasional stands of hardwoods. Water flowed from the height of land north to the Arctic through gently rolling country about 1,000 feet above sea level, and any high ground was seldom more than 400 feet above this figure.

The first people in the area made no lasting mark on the land. They shared the terrain with plentiful wildlife that, apart from man, feared only natural predators and unchecked forest fires generated by summer lightning strikes.

The aboriginal people who came to this lonely land sometime around 5,500 B.C. are the ancestors of the Northern Algonquins, of which area Cree and Ojibway are members. Their way of life and customs became more sophisticated over time, but until the arrival of Europeans, their tools were primitive and life was sustained solely by the bounty of the forest and waters. There is little surviving evidence of these early inhabitants of the Porcupine. Small stone and copper tools, and fragments of fire-darkened pottery found by campsites and burial grounds are all that remain. The early people's nomadic ways were a form of conservation, for one family covered about a hundred square miles and never stayed in one place long enough to deplete game and fur species. Lakes such as Papakomeka, Kenogamissi and Katoshaskepeko, and rivers such as Mattagami and Tatchikipika, were named by the first people of the Porcupine.

The early white visitors to this part of the North were explorers, traders and adventurers. The French soldier D'Iberville led Canada's first commando raid when he came north from Montreal in the spring break-up of 1686 to take the English forts on James Bay by surprise. He passed through the rich mineral areas of Temiskaming, Larder Lake and the Porcupine, but neither noticed nor had time to search for the riches which earlier explorers had unsuccessfully sought.

Exploration was dictated by the aims of commerce. The English came through Hudson's Bay and consolidated their position while waiting for trade to come to them. While the English used ocean-going ships as their lifeline, the French adopted the Indian canoe and fanned out from their bases on the St. Lawrence. Eventually the Hudson's Bay Company abandoned its solely coastal trading stance and met the French competitors on the waterways wherever there were Indians with furs to trade. In the Porcupine district, a fur-trade trail linked the Mattagami and Abitibi river systems. Westward, the traffic passed from Night Hawk and Frederick House lakes along the Porcupine River, Porcupine Lake, Pearl Lake and Miller Lake. In an easterly direction the trail passed from Frederick House Lake to a place on the Abitibi River near the site of modern Iroquois Falls. Hill's Landing, on the Porcupine River just north of Night Hawk Lake, was a popular stopping place for both Indians and traders. When the trade in furs eventually declined, the place ceased to be a rendezvous until its utility was discovered by goldseekers bound for the Porcupine.

The French built the first fur-trade fort in the area. Named Piscoutagamy, the Indian word for Night Hawk, or St. Germain to honour its founder, the fort opened in 1673 and lasted for about 12 years. The main role of this outpost had been to intercept the Indians before they could reach the English traders. After St. Germain was abandoned, the Hudson's Bay Company used the site for its own post, but later moved to the southeast shore of Lake Wartowaha, now Frederick House. A plaque marks the spot by the Ontario Northland tracks at Connaught. The fort was never an important one and was only open when trade volume warranted. The Frederick House post would have been forgotten were it not for a crime that had all the elements of a first-class thriller.

The small trading post at Frederick House had a staff of three in 1812. The master was a company servant and there were two labourers. All were under the authority of a larger post to the southwest at Lake Kenogamissi. Although fur-bearing animals were still plentiful, rabbits and fish were the staple diet not only of trappers but also the traders. When the rabbit cycle was low, starvation was a real threat, and these were lean years for those who lived in the bush.

Two of the Frederick House men left Kenogamissi on December 23 after picking up some trade goods. They may have carried with them some pudding, meat and brandy to celebrate Christmas, for the Hudson's Bay Company always provided some items for a feast at this time of the year. Richard Good, the master at Kenogamissi, heard no more from the outpost for three months. He was worried. He reasoned that the Frederick House men should be bringing in traded furs and have a need for more provisions and trade goods. When no such visit was forthcoming, he sent two men to Frederick House on March 23. They returned almost immediately with a horrifying story. All doors to the dwelling house, cellar and warehouse were either open or ripped from their hinges. The place was deserted, with no sign of the "residenters."

All guns were gone, and there were signs of robbery and destruction everywhere. The dogs, cats and poultry were missing. But it was in the men's quarters that the searchers had seen the sight which had made them hurry back in fear for their lives. An Indian and his wife were lying shot dead with their baby smothered beneath them. Due to the depth of snow, no other clues to the tragedy were found outside.

Relations between Company traders and the Indians were generally amicable. Good realized that he had a duty to keep the peace. After noting all the facts in his diary, he sent four men to investigate further. They were warned to be on sharp lookout for a possible ambush. Meanwhile, with his own post practically deserted, Good kept all guns in his quarters and loaded them against possible attack.

The investigators visited Frederick House and discovered the body of one of the three missing traders under a pile of casks in the servants' quarters. He had been shot to death. After burning their unfortunate colleague in a grave hacked out of the frozen ground, they returned with the only furs they had found in the abandoned post. These were of such poor quality that Good believed the prime pelts had been stolen. Most Company goods at the post were recovered. The party had hidden what they could not carry.

Post master Good notified his superior at Moose Factory and also the "Canadians" in the vicinity. These were members of the North West Company, the only serious rival to the Hudson's Bay Company. With the authority of his superior, Good offered a reward for the capture of the killers. Some traders felt this was a mistake, for it warned those responsible and might cause other Indians to close ranks and shelter the guilty ones.

Spring trading prevented any further investigation at the murder site, and it was not until June that Good's men were able to return. They found the other two Company servants some distance from the post, where they had fallen in December. Four murdered Indians were also located in different places around the buildings. All bodies were highly decomposed and picked over by passing animals. The stench was such that they were buried at once in shallow graves. A closer examination of the buildings revealed that all flour and dried goods had been taken, and it reinforced the view that the killers had been starving and had used the post for some time after the murders. Company records show that it was later determined that an Abitibi Indian, Capascoos, was the ringleader of the murderers. For the next few years word circulated to the effect that he had been seen travelling in the region, but he never personally visited any trading posts and the Indians were not willing to betray him.

The Company salvaged materials from the Frederick House post, and the place became overgrown and was forgotten for over 90 years. Then, in 1911, a steam shovel digging for road ballast for the new railway into the Porcupine brought up musket barrels, copper kettles and kegs. Not far away, several skeletons were discovered in shallow graves. Fifty years later Maggie Leclair, a well-known Indian figure from Kamiskotia, claimed to be descended from survivors of the massacre. She could have been, too, for a man and three children who had been at the post were never located. Today the site is marked only by a historical plaque. There is no other physical evidence of the place where at least ten people were murdered by the shores of Frederick House Lake.

The rest of the nineteenth century was quite uneventful in the Porcupine. The unification of the country in Confederation made no particular changes in that seldom-visited part of the continent. The only newcomers were white trappers who did not have the same conservation ethic as the Indian people. A decline in demand for raw furs and depleted populations from years of overtrapping caused the Hudson's Bay Company to close its trading posts. The lonely land was home only to the Indians, passing missionaries and occasional traders.

Towards the end of Queen Victoria's reign, the provincial government became more interested in the North Country. There was pressure for colonization both north and west of North Bay, and calls for a railway to open up land to the north. Such a line would not be practical unless it had freight traffic. There were rumours of land suitable for agriculture, and signs of minerals had been seen by travellers. More to satisfy critics than anything else, the government decided to map the North and take note of just what the country had to offer. With such a step, the isolation of the Porcupine would soon be over.

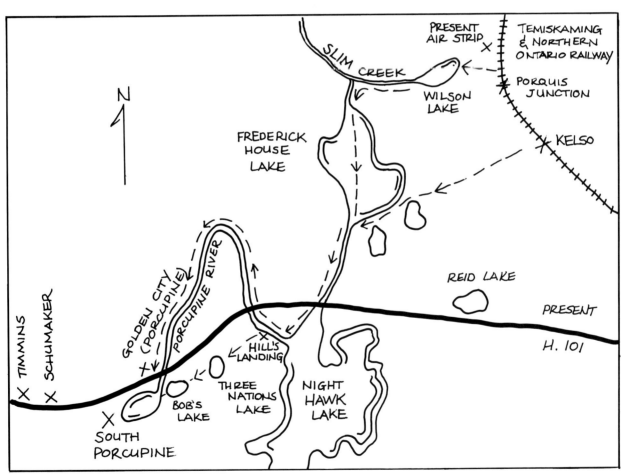

Prospectors' routes in to the Porcupine.

- Author

Reuben D'Aigle,the man who just missed finding the great Hollinger gold property, shortly before his death in 1959.
                                                                    - Toronto Star

CHAPTER 1

A Prospector's Story

There have always been prospectors in the Porcupine. Men still crisscross the area looking for precious and base metals. One of the great axioms of mining is that the game gives out even-handed chances. The romance lies in the story of lost opportunities. Reuben D'Aigle was one of the many who never did strike it rich, and yet his loss was so significant that his story should be remembered. He is the forgotten man of the Porcupine, the man who had a colossal fortune within his grasp and missed it by a boot print.

D'Aigle was a young man in the last decade of the nineteenth century. Like so many others, the young New Brunswick native was lured by the siren call of the Klondike. He suffered with other hopefuls on the six-month journey around South America. Not long after his arrival, he realized that the great Klondike gold camp was largely staked out.

D'Aigle differed from his fellow greenhorns in one important way: he was extremely stubborn and rarely gave up without a fight. While many disillusioned prospectors returned to the sea and took a boat home, D'Aigle travelled up the Yukon River into Alaska. There he prospected the Kayukuk, a tributary of the Yukon River. At Cleary Creek he found a gold camp starting up. Gold colours in the river looked good, and the young adventurer staked 30 claims. One of these became the richest in the camp.

When he sold out seven years later, D'Aigle had a big bankroll and so much gold that he had to trundle it to the waiting sternwheeler in a wheelbarrow. He hired guards to bring the precious cargo safely to the office of the United States mint. At this point D'Aigle's path diverged from the route taken by many successful prospectors of the time. He did not lose most of his fortune in a big spending spree. Instead D'Aigle looked for promising mining fields. Nothing out west took his interest, but he heard news of the silver boom at Cobalt.

The major ore bodies had been staked out, and D'Aigle saw himself as a mine-finder rather than a miner, so he left the area abruptly and went south to Kingston, Ontario. There was a novelty on the prospecting scene. Instead of hitting the bush until minerals could be seen underfoot, a prospector could go to Queen's University in Kingston and prepare with a short course in geology. D'Aigle felt he needed some formal instruction, as his only experience had been with rivers bearing placer gold, and deposits in the East were much different. The course was only of two weeks duration, so he felt he could spare the time. Outside of class, he could be found in the library, reading all the geology and survey reports. He noted one survey party's comment that gold-bearing rock had been observed in the Porcupine area of Northeastern Ontario. When the course was over, he packed his bush gear and headed north.

The new Temiskaming & Northern Ontario Railway was building beyond McDougall's Chutes, site of present-day Matheson. The logical approach to the Porcupine was to take a departure from somewhere on the line and travel overland. But D'Aigle rarely did things the easy way. With Métis companion Billy Moore, he took the Canadian Pacific Railway north to Mattagami, a tiny settlement 70 miles west of Sudbury. The whole area is veined with lakes and rivers. D'Aigle and his helper put their canoe in the Spanish River and paddled north to the Mattagami River, where they were able to drift leisurely down the waterway. Then the two portaged and paddled along a string of lakes between the Mattagami and a large lake called Porcupine (earlier visitors had noted that it resembled that solitary creature). They passed over what is now Miller Lake and then Delbert, today Gillies Lake. There was another short portage to Pearl Lake. No sign existed of any particular riches on its shores. They portaged for 1¾ miles and paddled for another mile, finally reaching the big Porcupine Lake.

The report written by government geologist W. Parks of Toronto had influenced D'Aigle's decision to come to this part of the northland. It was readily available in the university library but was not exactly a well-thumbed document. Parks had seen gold in the vicinity. D'Aigle scanned the lake and surveyed the area. There was rock everywhere. It lay underfoot, covered by moss, jutted out in bare clumps between the trees, and presented itself in many other forms. From unlined slabs to deeply crevassed outcrops, the ground offered a serious prospector plenty of work.

D'Aigle and Moore retraced the trail back to the Gillies Lake area, where a great knob of white quartz jutted up among the trees. D'Aigle and his partner scrambled about it in their hobnailed prospector's boots. There was visible gold and they staked seven claims, but somehow the gold that D'Aigle saw disappointed him. The quartz seemed to dwarf every other showing. The two men chipped some samples and went south. The specimens later showed promising results, but did not impress D'Aigle. Like so many other prospectors he was interested only in a spectacular find.

No one ever said that Reuben D'Aigle was a quitter. The next summer he drew on his Alaska gold earnings to finance an eight-man party into the Porcupine country. This time he took hand steel, blasting powder and even a small anvil. Several small pits were excavated, but there was none of the free gold of which the stubborn prospector dreamed. Bob Mustard, a seasoned bushman in the party, summed up their disappointment: "Quartz veins in Ontario never pay to work." The remark is a classic example of hapless misinformation, but at the time it made sense to Reuben D'Aigle. He agreed and they abandoned the Porcupine, leaving the steel and anvil in the shallow workings.

Reuben D'Aigle spent the rest of his life prospecting, until he was well into his seventies. He was to be the first in another great camp, the iron fields of Northern Quebec, but there too, he experienced the same disappointing results and lack of interest among the mining fraternity. His seven claims lapsed for lack of work and proper registration, and the moss grew up around his test pits. That neglect was too bad, because the moss covered a fortune. Reuben D'Aigle was never bitter about his losses. Before he died in 1959, he reflected on those Porcupine days: "I was there not a blame too soon. There's one thing about prospecting: you can never say you didn't have a chance."

The Triple Lake Mine, 1910, held promise but did not deliver and its location is not known today.

- John Kirwan, Timmins Museum

CHAPTER 2

First on the Ground

North of lakes Timiskaming and Abitibi, a long crescent of mineral-bearing rock stretches several hundred miles. Someone had to stumble across parts of it eventually. Even before a provincial railway was started north from North Bay, E.M. Burwash made a survey through the Porcupine for the Department of Mines. He found quartz veins bearing gold in Shaw Township, to the south of present-day South Porcupine, though strangely enough, no major gold finds have ever been located in Shaw. In 1898, 1899 and 1903 a University of Toronto geologist on contract to the province found gold-bearing rock in Whitney Township. On his trips, W. Parks crossed the ground which would become the Paymaster Mine and was close to what became the Dome, Broulan, Hallnor and Pamour properties. Reuben D'Aigle had read Parks' comment, "I regard the region south of the Porcupine trail as giving promise of reward to the prospector." Parks' colleague, Kay, was more pessimistic, saying, "No minerals of economic importance were found." Both men passed Miller Lake. Had they spent any time there at all, they would have found one of the Hollinger veins. But that particular treasure-trove had to wait a while longer.

Railways in Canada at the turn of the century were bold, aggressive enterprises. They actively sought freight as well as carried it. The Algoma Central Railway, with its headquarters at Sault Ste. Marie, was interested in iron ore. Iron meant progress and less of a reliance on American ore bodies, like those in the Mesabi Range. The railway hired a young geologist, Charles Camsell, to search for iron. In 1901 he travelled the Mattagami River from its source north of Sudbury right through to James Bay. He never did find iron, but on the way back he saw signs of another metallic element. Night Hawk Lake lay on the old Hudson's Bay Company route that he had followed. He was surprised to find evidence of claim-staking on one of its islands. The fact that some prospector was interested in the area piqued his professional curiosity. Camsell continued on to the Mattagami River. Portaging between Pearl and Miller lakes, he noticed quartz outcroppings. Some of the specimens he chipped off for later analysis in Sault Ste. Marie subsequently assayed at $5.20 gold to the ton, considered too low a return for active interest at the time.

People who talked of a major gold strike in Northern Ontario were bucking conventional mining wisdom. A gold rush in Lake of the Woods at the turn of the century had fizzled out and many felt that while gold was common in the North Country, it only appeared in small, non-commercial deposits. The coming of the T&NO, however, increased the chance of discovery of precious metals. By 1905 the line had extended beyond Cobalt, and the great silver discoveries around mile 104 brought the first precious-metal staking rush in Canada that was not based on gold. The new rail line through the northeast offered prospectors an easy means to reach deep into hard-rock country.

Prospectors know that gold is where you find it and untried country is as promising a place as any to look for it. All those fast-moving adventurers needed was a hunch and a grubstake to hit the trail. There were no fat men among them. They canoed and packed their way into the bush. The majority of these birds of prey could read a compass and follow a star. No record exists of those who failed and died in some unknown stream or deep in a dense swamp. Most lacked formal training. They knew some bush lore, and they knew that the presence of rocks meant the chance of veins which might contain minerals. Most just drifted into the life (surely no one consciously starts out to work in rough clothes, all exposed flesh smeared with fly dope almost as unpleasant as the bugs themselves and certainly more odorous). These loners knew how to mark out a 40-acre claim with a 1,320-foot side. They knew how many claims could be staked in a year, but rarely did the work necessary to patent them. They took the best deal offered and then headed out for the new Eldorado. They took the cash and let the credit go.

In the early years of the twentieth century, other men obtained an interest in the northland without ever going there. A grateful government decided to reward those who had seen active service for Canada. Soldiers who had served in the defence force against the Fenian raids across the international boundary in the 1860s, and those who had fought more recently in the Boer War, received veterans' land grants. Many never even saw the properties they received, but they sold them off later. Those who held on to them were often rewarded for their patience. In 1905 Simon Cotton belatedly received such a grant via the Crown Lands Department. A faded document describes the 160 acres he was granted in Whitney Township for his part in repulsing Fenian activity. No record exists as to

For several years, the canoe was the only transport to the Porcupine.

- H. Peters, Bob Atkinson collection

the final disposition of that property, but a few lucky recipients found that their grant covered promising ore-bearing ground.

A prospector named Edward Orr Taylor staked a claim on the southwestern shore of Night Hawk Lake as early as 1905 but could not sell the property. A wandering missionary, Father Paradis, crisscrossed the Porcupine country, but his brush with prospecting came later. Two Finns, Victor Mansen and Harry Benella, came next. They did not have the advantage of the railway and made the hard trip from the Abitibi River by following the same trail as the French adventurer D'Iberville. They found a gold-bearing vein on what became known as Gold Island in Night Hawk Lake. Gold was discovered there in 1906, and they recorded their claim the next year. Unlike many prospectors, they actually developed a little mine, rigged up a crude mill, and even produced a small bar of gold before fire put them out of business in 1908.

The railway was reaching northwards toward Cochrane, and it was inevitable that prospectors would use it to check out the stories of gold in the Porcupine. Charlie Auer was one of the first to leave the line just north of Matheson in 1907 and make his way by canoe and portage. He staked the property which became known as Night Hawk Peninsula. The mine was a slow starter but eventually produced half a million dollars in gold. In that same year A.G. Hunter of Toronto pushed on to Porcupine Lake and made a discovery on the east side, but it was 30 years before any worthwhile gold was recovered. Alex Kelso was working on the survey for the railway when he was bitten by the prospecting bug. He tracked down the old government reports of schist near the south boundaries of Tisdale and Whitney. Eventually, east of Night Hawk Lake, he discovered a large quantity of highly mineralized sulphide which turned out to be nickel. There was no urgent need for the metal, as Sudbury had an overabundance of it, but when war came the nickel deposit became "strategic." The resulting nickel mine and the business it brought delighted the railway, which named one station Kelso and the other Alexo, recalling the prospector.

Nickel and small gold finds could not keep prospectors in the Porcupine in 1908. There were rumours of strikes in Gowganda, new silver sources around Cobalt, and much unexplored ground between. It was not until June 1909 that George Bannerman and Tom Geddes made the strike that may be said to have started the Porcupine gold rush. Geddes had previously accompanied Hunter on his staking trip. Bannerman was a newcomer but destined to remain in the country he helped to develop. The two hopefuls worked over the ground to the north of Porcupine Lake, coming across old claims that had lapsed through lack of registration. One day their picks turned over fragments of rock that were shot through with visible gold. This was found to continue for some distance. With the ever-present prospector's fear that someone else might be close

at hand, they went without food and sleep to blaze out a 40-acre claim, and then two more for good measure. Even while they were hurrying off to Haileybury to record their find, "Hardrock" Bill Smith, Joe Vipond and Bill Davidson were all locating significant properties. The Bannerman-Geddes claims became the Scottish-Ontario Mine, then the Canusa, and finally the Banner, but it never did prove successful, as the ore petered out underground. But what turned out to be a disappointing discovery actually triggered a major gold rush.

Packers could carry up to 200 pounds in packsacks supported by tumplines round their forehead.   - OA 3843

19

Among the earliest stakers in the Porcupine were Clary Dixon, unknown, Alex Gillies and Tom Midleton.

- Teck Centennial Library

CHAPTER 3

The Mine Finders

Explorers, fur traders and surveyors had crossed the Porcupine for close to 200 years without finding a major gold strike. Prospectors had actively searched in the area for the past six years without great success. In 1909 three parties made discoveries that would establish the Porcupine as one of the major mining camps of the world.

Long-time prospector Jack Wilson worked on the railway as a construction foreman between financed trips for mineral exploration. In 1907 he stopped his handcar near Boston Creek to examine some gold-bearing rock. Although the samples looked good, he was not able to interest anyone further. In this way, he missed being in on the Boston Creek-Kirkland Lake camps. In 1908, after a bout of typhoid fever, Wilson quit his job when he found two Chicago businessmen, W.S. Edwards and Dr. T.N. Jamieson, who liked his prospecting style. Wilson was a firm believer in taking a sizable crew on such trips, as he felt it increased the odds of making a good discovery. He waited in the silver town of Cobalt for the $1,000 Edwards had promised him. The letter came, but to Wilson's former base camp at Driftwood, now Monteith. A blacksmith's shop there doubled as the post office, and Wilson's mail fell from the nail where it was spiked. Wilson languished in Cobalt until the letter was found in the spring.

In mid-May 1909 the Wilson party of seven left the railway at mile 228. The men included Harry Preston, Cliff and Frank Campbell, and George Burns. They took three canoes and worked their way by portage and paddle to the Porcupine, 15 miles to the west. Two weeks were spent mapping and prospecting, and they saw several traces of free gold. There were dome-like masses of quartz to the southwest of Porcupine Lake. They trenched the biggest dome, then Wilson made a brush broom and swept the trench clean. He examined the seams in the quartz, and then, about 12 feet ahead of his broom, he saw gold glisten as the sun struck it. "It proved to be a very spectacular piece of gold in a thin seam of schist," he recalled. "We got out the drills and hammers, and that night had about 132 pounds of specimens." The vein was traced and found to be several hundred feet in length and 150 feet wide.

Harry Preston later set off a dynamite blast in the quartz dome. The large vein plastered with gold became known as the Golden Staircase.

The yellow metal just hung down the hillside. An early visitor said: "The gold was in blobs like candle drippings, and in sponge-like masses, some of them as large as a cup, lying under the moss...the Big Dome, they called it." Wilson was careful to stake the allowable claims, for he had seen Geddes and Bannerman leave to record their claims and he knew a staking rush would follow. He left to wire his backers of their good fortune and quietly went and obtained new mining licences. They had exceeded their limit earlier, and the four claims that were to be the nucleus of the Dome Mine were not valid until the new papers arrived. He came back with Edwards, who had taken the train north as soon as he heard the news. They had an unfortunate start when Edwards, an extremely stout man, upset the canoe and was soaked. The backer forgot his damp condition on arrival at the camp, where he was able to feast his eyes on a veritable jewellery box in the crumbled rock.

The Dome deal was the most promptly concluded of the three great finds that summer. By the light of the campfire it was agreed that Jamieson and Edwards would receive half of the property in exchange for their backing and further assessment work. Wilson took ten percent and the other seven divided the remaining 40 percent. The settlement was topped with an additional $1,000 cash payment to each man. Harry Preston became disgruntled with his share, but a bottle of whisky placated him. The opening sentence of Wilson's telegraph from Driftwood the next day reflected the excitement of the group: "Have discovered the golden pole beyond description."

Benny Hollinger was a barber and his friend Alec Gillies was working cutting pulpwood. When news of the Bannerman and Wilson discoveries reached Cobalt, they found a grubstake for a prospecting trip. Gillies managed to get $100 from Jack Miller, while Hollinger's uncle, Jack MacMahon, the bartender at the Matabanick Hotel, added $45. The gold rumours fueled speculation in the silver town, and as soon as the pair left on their trip, the astute bartender sold half his share for $55 to Gilbert Labine.

Disappointment hit the two hopefuls when they finally packed into the Porcupine and were told at the Dome camp that most of the land to the west was taken. Wilson informed them that they would have to go at least

In this rare photograph, the investors stand on their gold vein at the Hollinger. From left Noah and Henry Timmins, Al Pare who persuaded his uncles to invest, and partners Dunlap, Bell, McMartin, unknown.

- Alphonsine Pare Howlett

4 miles further west to find open ground. They followed his suggestion and wound up near Pearl Lake. Right away they came across Reuben D'Aigle's rusty anvil and drill steel lying in the small pits where he had abandoned them. His excavations and the fact that the material had all been packed in did not discourage Gillies and Hollinger. The idea that someone had gone to such trouble made them more careful in their search.

Hollinger won a coin toss, so he staked first, while Gillies worked around him. They were out of sight of each other when Gillies heard a yell. "I was cutting a discovery post, and Benny was pulling off the moss some distance away, when he suddenly let a roar out of him and ran and threw his hat at me. At first I thought he was crazy,, but when I came over to where he was, it was not hard to find the reason. The quartz where he had taken off the moss looked as if someone had dripped a candle along it, but instead of wax it was gold. The quartz stood about three feet out of the ground and was about six feet wide with gold splattered all over it for about sixty feet along the vein."

No prospector stops to eat or rest when others could be coming up on his ground. Hollinger and Gillies staked their quota, but even in haste they still had time to do a good turn. One claim was for an old partner, now too crippled with sciatica to work in the bush. The one they reserved for Barney McEnaney later became the Porcupine Crown property and ensured he would never want for anything again. As they worked, both men noticed some impressions they had seen in the free gold. In one case a heel print was clearly visible. Reuben D'Aigle had tramped all over the area, maybe even sat where they sat now. Benny and Alec made their way out by land, water and rail to record their claims. A sample taken at the location of one boot mark assayed in extremely high values.

As Hollinger and Gillies were leaving their claims, two other prospecting groups met up with them. Clary Dixon, Tom Middleton and Jack Miller shared their excitement for a moment before shoving off to the west. In another canoe, two newcomers hardly paused before moving north across the lake. They reasoned that if a big strike had been made to the south of them, chances were that more gold might exist close by.

Sandy McIntyre and Hans Buttner are known mainly for the two claims they staked that evening. The claims would form the nucleus of the third great mine in the Porcupine camp, the McIntyre. Buttner was a quiet German immigrant, still learning English. He was an even-tempered man who only became annoyed when he was mistakenly referred to as "the Dutchman." McIntyre was perhaps the most colourful of the stakers, and he gained in fame rather than money, which ran through his fingers as fast as he made it. There are few good pictures of Sandy left, but the best ones show him on the trail, ready to hit the bush again. One shows him standing on snowshoes, axe handle clearly visible, ready for blazing a trail. The man acknowledged by his peers to be a superb bushman wears a half-open coat, and a battered felt hat sits jauntily on his head. A thick beard frames the face of a man who was better at searching for gold than at keeping it.

Sandy spoke well, but never said much about his early days in Scotland. His real name was Alexander Oliphant, and he was an itinerant moulder or patternmaker by trade. He had a wife with a shrill tongue, and after one argument too many, the restless Scot had abruptly taken passage for Canada, adopting his mother's maiden name and starting out fresh as McIntyre. He drifted into the prospector's life and in 1906 squatted at what is now Bourkes, south of Ramore. He called the place Scotty Spring. From there he prospected in Larder Lake, and his licence K51 came from that mining division. Since Hans Buttner's licence was 7283B from Haileybury, their association was likely a recent one.

After selling their shares back in Haileybury, Hans Buttner travelled and wisely saved his money. The two met again in 1913 and had a picture taken to recreate their staking, but then they split up, with Buttner returning for a while to his native Germany. As for Sandy, he sold a quarter of his interest for $300, then an eighth for $25, later a half for $5,000, and finally an option for $60,000, which he never collected. From that time forward the Scot's fortunes fluctuated and he was never really lucky again.

Noah Timmins joined the party in the first camp on the Hollinger, 1909. From the left.? Reid, Jim Labine, unknown, Alex Gillies, Noah Timmins and R.G. Campbell. - OA S3068-14

Alec Gillies and Benny Hollinger after they staked the nucleus of the great Hollinger Mine.

- OA-S3068-17

The Dome was the most promptly developed of the three great properties. The McIntyre property lay dormant for a long time, partly because Sandy clung to his shares and because there were no clearly ascendent backers. The development of the claims which were to become the great Hollinger Mine was largely due to the energy and enthusiasm of 24-year-old mining engineer Alphonse (Al) Pare. The Timmins brothers, Noah and Henry, held the Larose, the most prominent silver mine in Cobalt. Al Pare was their nephew and worked at the mine in summer months. He heard rumours of the Gillies-Hollinger find and went to the Porcupine with a friend, Johnny Sauvé, to see the new gold prospects for himself. He said later of the claims, "It was as if a giant cauldron had splattered the gold nuggets over a bed of pure white quartz crystals as a setting for some magnificent crown jewels of inestimable value."

Without even consulting his uncles, Pare tried to option the claims from Benny Hollinger. But young Hollinger told him that his uncle, Jack MacMahon, had power of attorney. Pare borrowed Benny's samples and from Matheson wired Noah Timmins to meet him in Haileybury. There he had no trouble convincing one uncle of the value of the property. While Noah was enthused, Henry backed out. "Alphonse," he said, "you have ruined your Uncle Noah." The younger man was positive and replied correctly, "No, I'm making him a great fortune."

Noah Timmins could see the potential of the Porcupine ground but could not convince his partners, John and Duncan McMartin, David Dunlap and his brother Henry. This would come later. In the meantime he dickered with the happy Matabanick bartender MacMahon for 120 acres of rockbound bush, and finally secured ground worth a king's ransom.

The three men Hollinger and Gillies left behind also took ground which would make mines. Out of their work came the Middleton and Coniaurum. Jack Miller, who was a backer in addition to being in on the staking, became a millionaire on the strength of a $100 investment.

By October 1909 all the initially promising ground was staked. The news of the Hollinger, Dome and McIntyre discoveries had leaked to the outside world. The isolation was over. The gold rush to the Porcupine was on.

Silver bars at Kidd Creek.

- Don Thompson collection

Heads bowed from the tumpline round their foreheads which steadied the big loads, these men headed for the Porcupine. Note the tea pail on one pack. The lead man stopped and took this picture.
- Author collection

CHAPTER 4

Building the Camp

Roughly two years of hard work built up the Porcupine gold camp. As ever, the geologists and mapmakers followed the prospectors. They found that one of the reasons the ground had kept its secrets well hidden was that it was much altered and metamorphosed. The rock which made the camp consisted of great flows of lava, dacite, andesite and, rarely, basalt. Cyril Knight first mapped the Hollinger property and at times found it difficult to draw boundaries between the intrusive porphyry and the basic lavas. He noticed D'Aigle's original pit in the heart of the Hollinger veins, mute testimony to one man's bad luck.

With the three great properties as an anchor to the camp, lesser mines were developed with the communities of Golden City, Pottsville, South Porcupine and Aura Lake to serve for both residence and commerce. The gold-bearing area was found to be 3 miles wide and 5 miles long, and gold mines have produced there ever since.

The deal Noah Timmins made with Jack MacMahon for the Hollinger claims was believed to have been worth $330,000, but this has never been established. Alec Gillies received $90,000 and Benny Hollinger around $150,000. The young barber-turned-prospector could have taken shares with the chance of becoming a multi-millionaire, but he could not wait for his reward for staking the property. As it was, all funds were dispersed in instalments as Timmins borrowed the money to purchase the property before his old partners rejoined him. Next came a trip to see the claims and commence development. Noah, Alphonse Pare and 28 men left from the railway after freeze-up in December. Camps were set up, and it was found that old lumber roads could be used on the way to Night Hawk Lake. Two teams of horses hauling freight for the party ploughed through the snow to the big lake. There was still only 2 inches of ice, and even with rearranged loads the teamsters were not happy with the route. Several trips were made, during which the horses broke through the ice a dozen times. At the end of it, there was a 20-mile passage to Pearl Lake, but they had a rough road opened by New Year's Day 1910.

From that point, and for two years, Al Pare was in charge of the operation. As they sat by a campfire one night, he astonished his uncle by nailing to a tree a board with the name "Timmins" scratched on it. This was to be the community that would grow up dependent on the mine they intended to build. Noah was flattered and the name stuck. The majority shareholder worked right along with the men for some time as they cleared land, built cabins and did initial shaft work, but had returned to the financial end of things by March, when there were 125 men working on-site. Pare prudently had the first mill and office built right over the rich surface veins. He was afraid of high-grading and knew that the buildings would be replaced as the mine developed and the surface gold could be worked more securely.

Jack Miller had optioned his claims in the Gillies property (now called the Acme) to industrialist M.J. O'Brien. The latter had operated a silver mine in Cobalt. His agreement called for $200,000 in a series of payments, and he could withdraw from this agreement if not satisfied with the results. He instructed his engineer, Culbertson, to do some drilling before the initial payment was due. This was done, but because of a heavy load, Culbertson discarded those samples that did not carry quartz. Assay results were poor and O'Brien dropped his option. That was too bad, because the discarded samples carried the real values.

Timmins acted quickly when he heard that financier Ambrose Monell of the Dome had offered double O'Brien's deal, although in smaller payments. Timmins countered with less ($350,000), but in much larger amounts than Monell had tendered. It was at this point that Timmins' Cobalt partners rejoined him and Wilson took the deal. In a short time the Timmins interests acquired the 560 acres that made up the Hollinger, Miller, Gillies, Millerton and Acme claims. The total purchase price was a record for gold properties at the time. One million dollars secured a mining empire. The Hollinger was incorporated at $3 million, comprising 600,000 shares at $5 each. Over the next 58 years the mine produced 19.3 million ounces of gold and paid $564,700,000 in dividends.

Just a few months after the Timmins expedition into the Porcupine, travellers left the train at Kelso. There was no station, but at least there was a place to stop overnight (such spots were too rough to be called hotels). At 7 AM a wagon left for Frederick House. This connected with a boat which crossed the lake and followed its river to Hill's Landing. So far the trip had cost $3.50. A meal could be purchased at Hill's Landing –

In spring the way to the Porcupine was a morass of mud and muskeg.   - Author collection

already a stopping place for more than 150 years. One then proceeded on foot to Three Nations Lake. One traveller remarked, "This road was much different from the other northern roads inasmuch as it was uniformly bad all the way. It was a simple arithmetical deduction. The road was all clay; that northern clay is pure hell when it's wet; the road was always wet." A hired boat across the lake led to another 2-mile hike to Bob's Lake. After another ferry ride, a mile jaunt brought the by now thoroughly sore and bedraggled travellers to Golden City. (The roads in from Hill's Landing were later improved by prisoners from provincial jails.)

The gold-streaked Dome did not find a buyer as promptly as the Hollinger. W.S. Edwards set up shop in Toronto's King Edward Hotel, but investors were slow to beat a path to his door. Among those who came to hear about the property and later see it on the ground was Captain Joseph Delamar, a scout for financier Ambrose Monell, who had ties to the International Nickel group in Sudbury. Monell accepted the report, and the Dome was purchased and assured of strong financial backing. The gold was so rich at surface that the mine started in the fall of 1910 as an open-pit operation. Armed guards protected the exposed gold. There were the usual critics who felt the precious metal would peter out when it went underground, and Harry Preston, who tended to think of it as *his* mine, became agitated at the prospect. He had no cause for alarm. Directors included Jack Wilson, W.S. Edwards and Dr. Jamieson,

but the company was controlled by American financial interests from the start. As well as Monell and Delamar (called "Hard Cash," for that was his sole method of payment), "Handsome" Charlie Dennison (so called because his features were quite the opposite), was one of the principals. All inherited ground the glaciers had spared. Had the area been eroded another 150 feet, there would have been no rich quartz knob. It disappeared anyway, at the 200-foot level, and the mine went underground. Share capitalization of $2.5 million was achieved by a pricey $10 per share. They took in 214 ounces of gold and 19 of silver that first year, and the mine still operates.

Though a great mine, the McIntyre took two years to establish ownership. It did not have the surface lure of the Dome and Hollinger. Hans Buttner didn't wait around to see how things went. As for Sandy McIntyre, he stayed until he had lost most of what he made on his great discovery. The property went through Charles Flyn, A. Freeman, and finally J.P. Bickell. The latter put together the ground which would stand as the main property, and when it was incorporated in 1912, only two of McIntyre's original claims were included. Share capital of $3 million was achieved by selling shares at $1. Sandy had no further interest in the place. At one point before the big mine was established, it could actually have been purchased for $90,000. The Timmins interests had done business with a British firm, Berwick Moreing, and suggested the two compa-

Golden City prior to 1911 looked like cow towns of the U.S. West but lacked the violence.

- OA S13714

Today Golden City has given way to Porcupine but the street angle to the lake is the same.

- OA S13713

Shacks and stumps summed up the first town in the Porcupine.

- Author collection

nies form a partnership. If the British had purchased the McIntyre, the Timmins group would have added adjacent claims and it could have been worked jointly. The offer was declined, and Noah Timmins said just before he died that in doing so the British principals had passed up the chance to be many millions of dollars richer.

As the Porcupine grew, it was obvious that the place needed some form of municipal direction. Sylvester Kennedy was one of the first builders in South Porcupine. He chose a likely spot for his house, but later surveyors found he had located it right in the middle of Golden Avenue, so he obligingly relocated to the edge of the street. No proper development, even at this modest level, could be undertaken until high transportation costs were cut. Right up to the spring of 1911, the stage-coach and boats were the only means of entry to the camp. Freight expenses were reflected in higher wages at the new mines. Surface workers received a premium $2.50 a day, while underground miners took home 50 cents more. The sheer number of men working in mining in mid-1910 prompted the province to build a road from Hill's Landing to Golden City, again using much convict labour. As the new year opened there were 50 stages operating into the gold camp, but their utility would come to an end in six months.

Energetic T&NO chairman Jake Englehart had ordered a full-scale survey of a rail link with the Porcupine. The projected line was to cover 30 miles and leave the main line just north of Kelso. The province was in agreement and Porquois Junction became the entry point by rail to the Porcupine. The price tag was $450,000, and despite winter construction and manpower shortages, the steel reached the Frederick House River by April 1 and Golden City by June 7, 1911. At the official opening on July 1, Canada's birthday, invited guests stared soberly at the camera to record the event. As Englehart toasted both the railway and the new mining camp, neither he nor his audience realized that most of man's accomplishments in the Porcupine would soon by wiped out in a five-hour conflagration.

At the Dome Mine they took surface gold via this 'glory hole' before the workings went underground.   - John Kirwan, Timmins Museum

Snow was simply cleared, not removed, in the early days of the gold camp.
                                    - OA 3637-115

The shaft was sunk next to the quartz outcrop at this unknown Tisdale mine in 1910.   - PA 45233

FIRE IN PORCUPINE
JULY 11/11

H. PETERS
PHOTO

- Bob Atkinson collection

CHAPTER 5

Black Tuesday

In July 1911 a five-hour reign of terror wiped out two years of progress in the new gold camp. Few clues exist now concerning the fire that levelled the Porcupine. Look for them in roadside plaques, museums and cemeteries. The Timmins Museum has seven silver coins on display. Visitors take the number on faith, for they are little more than one silver blob. Consider that silver has a melting point of 962°C and some idea emerges of the force that brought the camp a few short hours of hell. There is a plaque outside Northern College, but many of the graves have been lost and most of the survivors are gone now.

The Temiskaming & Northern Ontario Railway rails reached South Porcupine on July 1, 1911. Much development had taken place in the two years since the three major properties were discovered. To obtain a fast return on investment, corners had been cut and conservation was not in the local lexicon. Roads into the camp had been brushed out and the slash left where it landed. Trees had been felled for corduroy roads, culverts and bridges, and the stumps and tops littered the land. The shacks and cabins in the gold camp villages that made up the Porcupine stood like islands in a sea of stumps. The mines were situated in tiny clearings in the bush. Cut wood was piled everywhere. Required for commercial buildings, houses and the railway, the tree fuel was essential in the development of the camp, and yet it was a time bomb waiting for its moment in history.

Porcupine Lake was the centre of the camp. The first village was Golden City, known today as Porcupine. It was on the north end of the lake. A short distance away, across the present causeway, was Pottsville. At the "South End" – still a common name for the town – was South Porcupine, the biggest settlement. The mines ran from the Dome, a mile from South Porcupine, up to the McIntyre and Hollinger, some 8 miles away. The former would be the site of Schumacher and the latter, Timmins. By the summer of 1911, 3,000 people lived in these townsites, which were supported by the activity of at least two dozen mining companies.

Winter snowfall had been lighter than usual and the spring melt of 1911 had been brief. Summer was hot across Canada, with record highs of 110°F in some places. The heat and tinder-dry bush did not deter settlers from using fire to clear land. Some burns grew out of control, and smoke could always be seen somewhere that summer.

Fire struck the camp on May 19. Workers cutting out lots for the new townsite of Timmins saw the Hollinger Mine go up in flames. A month later, as the Hollinger was receiving new machinery to rebuild the property, another fire hit the Dome Extension Mine and part of Pottsville. There was no undue alarm, as fire was seen as a normal part of northern life. The first ten days of July brought a heat wave, with small fires burning in Bristol, Deloro, Whitney and Tisdale townships. A fire threatened the Dome, and only the efforts of all 200 workers saved the property. South Porcupine people became alarmed as the mine was only a mile away. Sunday, July 9 was the fifth day of high winds and record temperatures. The next day another fire in Pottsville kept all able-bodied men passing buckets of water to save the community. People in the three communities began piling their belongings outside or on docks. On that Monday smoke was everywhere and flames could always be seen close by. The Cobalt *Daily Nugget* correspondent commented that rain was the only thing that would stop the bush fires.

In one of the many fires that plagued the area earlier, Bob Hatch, manager of the Foley-O'Brien Mine, played a fringe role. He enjoyed baseball and liked to watch the mine team versus a district club. He used his $200-a-month pay as manager to bet on the mine team. Caught up in the thrill of a contest, Hatch ignored an approaching fire. He won the bet, but the mine burned. Hatch rationalized that jobs could be found anywhere, but there was only one game and the mine would have likely burned anyway. Fortunately the shareholders never did hear the real story.

The residents of Canada's newest boom area went about their business while the fire that was to be the district nemesis developed close by. The place the southern papers called the Klondike of New Ontario was generally a quiet camp. Provincial Constable George Murray kept the peace at South Porcupine, while Charlie Percy patrolled Golden City. Both men were aware of Pottsville's log Shunia Hotel (an Indian word for gold), which sold liquor after hours like most hostelries, but the constables did not interfere if discretion was used.

Downed power cables were found at every mine site.   - OA S 13756

FIGHTING FIRE
PORCUPINE.
LAST STAND AT
ROWELLS POINT.

- Timmins Museum

A weatherman at Haileybury wrote "gale" as a forecast for Tuesday, July 11, 1911, and his prediction was right for the Porcupine. A breeze, which was at first welcomed as relief from the heat, quickened into a wind conservatively estimated to have had speeds of 70 miles an hour. Trees snapped, Porcupine Lake was whipped into a lather, and consolidating bush fires brought darkness at noon. The Dome staff were called to fight fire at 1:15 PM. The men fought a hopeless battle against flames that leapfrogged the trees. The roar was not unlike that of a steam train going flat out. The simile is appropriate, for like a train, the fire would take a great deal to stop, and indeed, within 20 minutes, it roared into South Porcupine.

Bob Weiss, the captain of the West Dome Mine, decided at first to fight the fire. His legendary 440 pounds, spread over a 6-foot-7 frame, stuck in barbers' chairs and tested the wagons he used. He reassured his wife and small daughter before directing mine efforts against the fire. Former heavyweight boxer Jack Munroe watched the fire from over in Golden City. He decided that the key to survival would be in organization of firefighting efforts. J.P. Bartleman, later mayor of Timmins, went out and dug a trench by his house to take valuables. John Campsall was only nine years old but had survived three major bush fires. Charlie Richardson was out in the bush with a prospecting crew. He had the men bury their gear and make for the lake. As he retrieved his trunk from Pottsville he remarked, "By this time I had dragged that luggage out of the way of fires so often it got so it would follow me!"

The two provincial constables watched while women and children took gas launches from South Porcupine to Golden City and men doused buildings with water. Those who stayed in "South End" spent the time in various ways. Carter Jack Dalton ran his wagons into the lake. Imperial Bank manager M.H. Mackay put all funds in suitcases and ferried them to safety in a canoe. Cliff Moore of the King George Hotel gave out cigars, which he decided might as well be smoked as burned. Storekeeper Billy Gohr stated plainly that he would lose everything if his store went, and in that event, "I might as well go too."

The fire was now horseshoe-shaped. The flames extended for 20 miles and in some places climbed to 150 feet. Edith Forsyth left with her dog for the safety of Golden City. Her husband Jimmy stayed to support his partner Tom Geddes in their claim-trading business. The two soon realized their efforts were useless against the fire, and the men of the Dome Mine were coming to the same conclusion. Flames could be seen shooting twice as high as the trees. Men broke and ran for their lives, but ten stayed and paid the price for their diligence. The plant was destroyed and at last the steady warning whistle was silenced. But there was no stop to the rush of wind and loud explosion of flaming tree trunks.

John Campsall recalled the flotilla of refugees fleeing across the lake. His mother put blankets in a dry well and covered them with a bag of flour. They stopped from time to time to remove burning embers from clothing. The constables checked to see that women and children had left, but Mrs. Gohr refused to go, preferring to wait in the water for Billy. People dotted the lake for a hundred yards out, where the water shelved steeply. Horses stood with their owners. The watchers in the lake could still see bucket brigades working frantically. The brigades only gave up when the temperature reached 118°F.

Two men wrestled a visiting harpist's instrument to the lake, but were forced to abandon it. Cap Dunbar was last seen manning a pump. His charred body was found by the handle after the fire. Bank of Ottawa manager Hawley Clayton borrowed a shovel from Henry Joy's store to bury the bank's precious ledgers. He told Joy the bank would pay him if he was still in business the next day.

Meanwhile, out in the bush, men and animals fled the fire. Several were surrounded by the flames. Some made it out and others were engulfed. John Novack's dog thought he should guard an abandoned sweater and was later found alive but with the pads of his feet burned off. One man escaped by pumping a rail handcar to Porquois Junction. Firefighters there were charmed to see a priest sprinkling the ground with water from a bowl. The fire seemed to abate at that point, and the men threw their shovels into the air and quit.

Over at the West Dome, the site now covered by the Paymaster Mine, Bob Weiss realized the property was doomed. While some miners made their way to South Porcupine, 17 others joined Weiss and his wife and daughter, using the bucket to go down the shaft to escape the circling fire. One miner, as he left, heard Weiss say to his wife, "You're not afraid, are you?" The West Dome was a new development, and the shaft was only 80 feet deep. First the surface plant was destroyed, then the flames reached down the shaft, destroying the large beams for a depth of 30 feet. But the force of the fire sucked all the oxygen out of the shaft. All those below died of asphyxiation in the greatest single tragedy of the fire. With all hoisting equipment destroyed, removing the bodies the next day was a difficult task.

There were various stories of survival. Some residents simply outran the wall of flames. Others sought areas which were open and had nothing to feed the fire. At the Dome water pond, a group of miners stood in water up to their necks while the mill burned. In Porcupine Lake, wind-whipped waters made it difficult to stand for several hours, and at least seven people just slipped under the water. Others stood and stared helplessly at the destruction of their town. Jack Munroe, for one, did not stand still. Golden City survived, and Munroe was acclaimed as the one who had successfully organized the bucket brigades around town. Refugees congregated at the spot known as Bannerman's Park. They were a sorry-looking bunch, most having escaped with only the clothes they

- MNR

- Bob Atkinson collection

wore. James Brooke was a survivor. He was among five men in a canoe built for three. Billy Moore and another man drowned when the vessel tipped.

No confirmation exists for the story of the woman who gave birth in the lake at the height of the fire. But the last words of the duty railway telegrapher have been preserved. His terse Morse phrases read: "Fire has taken possession of the town...very hot...smoke so thick I can hardly read...will close." The last train had gone, but a boxcar packed with 350 cases of dynamite went up. It was located on a siding built over a swamp, so some of the blast was cushioned, but the force of the explosion churned the wind-swept lake even further. Andy Leroux's boat was turned over and he drowned. One man lost his arm when a jagged piece of steel arced through the air and struck him. Glass was broken in Golden City, 2 miles away. The railroad track and cars on it were obliterated for 300 feet, and a crater 15 feet deep and 47 feet across was gouged out of the roadbed. This was fortuitous, for a spring welled up from the crater and provided fresh water for some time afterward.

The Porcupine and the town of Cochrane were wiped out. Eleven mines were destroyed. All buildings in South Porcupine, Pottsville and Aura Lake were razed. Property damage was estimated at $73 million. The official count was 73 dead. Speculation went higher than this figure, for it was believed that many had died in the bush without witness.

A cleansing rain eased the parched land two days later. Prospectors put the catastrophe in a positive light. In some areas the fire would have cleared the land down to bedrock and maybe would reveal new veins. It was a different story for the claims office. There had been 8,000 registered claims before the fire, and with the markers gone, a legal nightmare was created for harried mining recorders.

In the aftermath of the fire, ash was ankle deep in places and muskeg was burned down to a depth of 18 inches. The new T&NO Railway branch lost 4 construction camps, 40 telegraph poles and 60 crossarms. Plant and rolling stock were wiped out, but the South Porcupine station and freight shed survived. Line chairman Jake Englehart was placed in charge of provincial relief efforts. A week after the fire, the Northern Fire Relief Committee raised $37,000 in the Toronto area alone. The T. Eaton Company sent tents, blankets, clothing and stoves. One firm sent a thousand loaves of bread. The Dominion government sent tents and police to help work out relief and other problems. Survivors were given free time on the telegraph to contact anxious relatives. In the town named after him, Englehart tacked a poster on the station wall: "No one need pass here hungry."

As relief trains moved north, the people of the Porcupine picked up the threads of their lives. Some left the fire-ravaged area never to return. John Campsall's mother found her hastily buried blankets burned where fire had coursed down through the parched earth. Tom Geddes had paid

His home may have gone but the flames actually cleared many veins and presented new hopes for mines.
- Timmins museum

the supreme price when he returned for his coat. Jimmy Forsyth found his partner's remains in the shell of their building. Billy Gohr never did meet up with his wife, for he perished on the way. Some were found in the bush where the flames had overtaken them. Pottsville bank manager Hawley Clayton set up for business the next day in a saloon. There was much unclaimed mail at Aura Lake, and this gave rise to the belief that many more had died than were noted in the official tally.

Fire victims were shipped out to their home towns for burial, some as far afield as the Maritimes and the United States. Edward's Point, across the lake, seemed inappropriately named once the new cemetery was located there. The name Deadman's Point caught on, and it remains thus today. Seventeen rough boxes were interred. Bob Weiss and his family were buried in a single plot. Sadly, many markers were just rough boards and later rotted away. The majority of victims were buried near mine sites where they had worked. Since these mines have all gone now, their resting places are lost in the ever-encroaching bush.

Despite the fire, the railway pushed on to the new Timmins townsite and reached it a month later. (When Timmins was incorporated in 1912, one of its first acts was to purchase a fire engine. Ironically, the building which housed it burned soon after.) The Hollinger and Dome mines were rushed back into production, for their owners realized the potential of the properties. A year after the fire the Hollinger had a 200-ton-a-day

mill and recovered $900,000 in gold that first year. As for the Dome, the second day after the fire, president Ambrose Monell and other directors came north to the Porcupine by private railcar, then travelled by handcar, and finally walked to the fire-ravaged site. Monell went back to plan for a new plant, and within six weeks 500 men were working on reconstruction.

The Department of Lands and Forests concluded that blame for the fire could not be fixed on anyone in particular. Mines, towns and the people who worked for them all played a part. One unexpected bonus was that only jack pine and spruce burned and no valuable timber was lost. It was concluded that the great fire had gutted 500,000 acres or 781 square miles. The $3-million damage estimate was certainly low, for the loss at the Dome alone was one-sixth that sum. Today visitors to Deadman's Point will note a large concrete slab over the grave of the Weiss family. Nearby stands a granite pillar with a simple message: "Erected by the citizens of Canada through the Northern Ontario Fire Relief Committee with the Board of Trade of the City of Toronto to those who suffered and lost their lives in the great holocaust that swept this district, July 11, 1911."

The lasting monument to the Porcupine is the nature of the people and the towns that grew up within it. The five-hour reign of terror that took place on that Tuesday in July could not erase such tenacious northern settlers and settlements.

Somewhere near present day Bannerman Park, those who escaped the fire look back on the flames.   - Bob Atkinson collection

Sadly many survivors dug up belongings to find the fire had in some cases reached into the ground to destroy articles.

- Bob Atkinson collection

There was no shortage of work at the Dome after the fire.

- Timmins Museum

Timmins was new and raw in 1912.

CHAPTER 6

Recovery

The *Mining Journal* of London, England, gave its readers rotten advice in 1911. It declared: "The history of gold mining in Canada has been one of financial failure; and...caution should be exercised regarding the Porcupine field." Yet within 18 months of the great fire, recovery was complete, the camp was reestablished, and a new town had been founded.

Weeks after the fire, facts were still coming to light. No complete list of the conflagration's damage has ever been published, but a partial one referred to graves on the northeast side of Porcupine Lake, Deadman's Point and to victims buried at mines like the Dome, Pearl Lake, Porcupine Gold, Foley-O'Brien and United Porcupine Gold. Some of these injured died in transit, at the New Liskeard and Copper Cliff hospitals.

The fire also killed some corporations, and several marginal operations were never rebuilt. The East Dome was destroyed and stayed a hole in the ground for 23 years. But with gold at $12.51 an ounce, there was enough optimism in the industry to support any worthwhile venture.

Golden City became Porcupine, with a bank, a mining recorder's office, and services for all, including a building which proclaimed, "Meals and Stabeling" [sic], ready to serve man and beast.

The village fell into decline when it was not intersected by the new railway, and the Scottish-Ontario mine failed. Pottsville was absorbed into South Porcupine. It was on the wrong side of the lake to compete for traffic, as the wagon road was on the south side of the lake for many years until the modern highway was constructed. So "South End" grew, and for more than a year saw rapid construction of both houses and stores.

Fred Connell owned two former veteran's lots. The sand-covered ground ran from west of Miller Lake to the Mattagami River. Noah Timmins bought the property for a townsite for his work force. Many mining towns grew in haphazard fashion, but Timmins was confident the Hollinger would grow and operate for many years. He believed the miners would be content if they could own their own homes and bring up their families. He formed the Timmins Townsite Company for this purpose, and the first auction of lots took place on Labour Day 1911. Third Avenue was designated as the main street because the railway would soon arrive there. The mine owner built a substantial hotel, the Goldfields. Later he erected company houses. Building lots 30 by 90 feet went for $5 to $10, while commercial properties started at $75. Budding entrepreneur Charles Pierce borrowed $1,500 from Noah Timmins to buy three prime lots, then hit his benefactor again for a like sum to erect a store.

The pioneer settlers were a mixed bunch. Dayton Ostrosser saw his store at Pearl Lake wiped out in the fire. He went south to get credit, came back and later built in Timmins. His son Henry recalled that his father never forgot his loss in the fire. Every anniversary of the event he would take out his pocket watch and use it to remind all of the devastating event. Harry Peters by contrast had no reason to regret the fire. The struggling photographer's business was established with the sale of pictures he took on July 11, 1911, and over the following days. Leo Mascioli was 35 when he arrived during the Porcupine's year of recovery. Involved in both provision of labour and construction, the results of his work are seen all over the area today. Johnny Jones was a prospector who worked in the Porcupine from 1911 forward. He never made a good strike, but he endeared himself to people by his friendly nature. Even a dog figured as an occasional visitor. Cobalt, a bulldog from the silver town, would sometimes ride the trains. He would stop off for a while, leave his mark, and then, with train crew help, make his way back to Cobalt.

There were characters like Foghorn Macdonald, Texas Steve and Bacon Rind King. One entrepreneur ran a greenhouse. The market-garden operation was nicknamed the White Rat and really dispensed booze. Jack Shields was an early mail carrier who boasted of his strength. He may have been able to carry a loaded mail sack for 2 miles without putting it down, but once, when pranksters filled his load with scrap metal, Shields' prowess was sorely tested. Caroline Maben Flower was the first woman prospector. She never found the golden rainbow, but with her elegant outfit and holstered pistol, she added colour to a hard-luck profession. Jack Dalton ran the stage and livery service. He said the roads might be rough, but "with push and perseverance we could always swear our way through." Another character who appears in the Porcupine story is Maggie Leclair. The Indian woman was born on the shores of Night Hawk Lake in 1866, never saw a white man until she was 15, and after her first husband died, she lost all four children at once to childhood

Railway Chairman Jake Englehart speeded relief trains.　　　- Imperial Oil

The prospectors left for the bush as soon as the fire was over for they felt some veins would have been uncovered.　　　- Timmins Museum

Golden City became a tent community for refugees.　　　- PA 30023

- Bob Atkinson collection

*The Hollinger Mine provided single
family homes later.*

- Bob Atkinson collection

PEARL LAKE   SCHUMACHER TOWNSITE   BUNK-HOUSE   CLUB-HOUSE   McINTYRE GOLD MINE   SHAFT   STAMP-MILL

H.PETERS PHOTO

Nothing from this scene at Pearl Lake survives today.   - Bob Atkinson collection

diseases. Since she lived in an isolated spot, she buried them and was the sole mourner.

The railway was a life line for the Porcupine and would serve as the only link with the south for 16 years, until a road connection was made with Toronto. There was twice-daily train service in and out of the camp. T&NO lines were used by 21 private rail cars in March 1912, when directors and guests of the Dome came to celebrate a new spur line to the mine and the rebuilt property. A big "smoking concert" highlighted the event. Jake Englehart smiled with satisfaction at the ensured business for the line. The potted plants which decorated the hall came from the railway greenhouses at Englehart. The visitors found the roar of the 40-stamp mill music to their ears. The mill produced 400 tons a day in the first year, recovering almost $1 million in gold and providing a profit of $500,000.

W.H. Wilson was the first mayor of the new town of Timmins, which was incorporated January 1, 1912. The veteran's lots that Noah Timmins had bought were put to good use. Many such lots, if they had no mining potential, were never taken up and either remained as bush or later provided feed for the sawmills. Timmins was on a well-drained gravel ridge, safely above the Mattagami River flood plain. Dams at both Wawiatin and Sandy Falls provided power for both mine and residential properties. (The Cobalt camp, by contrast, had waited for years for a reliable power source. The hospital started first as a Hollinger company unit, later to be called Providence, after the order of nuns that staffed it. Fire service was strictly voluntary. The department had only a $5,000 steamer pump and a few hand reels to serve a population of 974. Citizens winced when the firemen's storage shed burned. A Roman Catholic church was built. Charlie Pierce added to his property, purchasing more lots as he had funds. He could boast that he was the first merchant – in a tent.

The paper of record was the *Porcupine Advance*. Most headlines were of mining news, but it was a lively paper with a breezy mix of fact, opinion and advertising. One August 1912 issue advised that $68,000 worth of gold was being produced in the area per month. An editorial opined that there was no need for a jail, as justice was swift, unless the building under construction was to provide people to shelter from their creditors. An indignant note from the Majestic Theatre averred that its pictures did not flicker. The paper reported without comment an account of exploration on the Moose River which talked of the discovery of rubies, garnets and even a diamond. No one has ever found the spot. Claims were offered for sale on every page, while panoramic pictures bore evidence to the town's raw nature, with tree stumps shown everywhere.

The prospectors moved on as the camp became settled. There were always new rumours, new hopes of free gold. The Porcupine camp had the regulated life of a hard-rock mining camp at depth once the surface

The salesman was as interested in his gold samples as in selling buildings.
- Timmins Museum

Timmins fire hall and chief.
- OA S 15380-78

gold had been quarried off. The average monthly wage was $80 to $85, and for 60 cents a day, full board was provided. The price for gold moved to $12.67 an ounce in 1912 and stayed at that figure for years.

At first the Vipond was the biggest producer, but it was soon overtaken by the Dome and Hollinger. Alphonse Pare stepped down as manager of the latter mine by year's end. The mine needed more experienced leadership as the plant became more complex. Pare was wealthy at 26 from the shares he had received, and he went away to visit Australia. Among the small companies which appeared to flourish was the Porcupine Twin Mine. A surviving photograph shows many buildings and much activity, yet within four years it was gone, a victim of overly optimistic ore claims. There were many mines like it.

The early days of the McIntyre were difficult. There was no guiding hand of a Timmins to sort out financial troubles. There were problems with the ore. Promising veins turned out to dip in and out of the Hollinger. Mill circuit flow took considerable time to adjust, and five shafts were sunk before a good ore body was established. There were many hard-luck tales of the mine's first years. Any firm that offers the company doctor shares in payment of his account must have had some difficulty. The first production year only achieved gold production to the tune of $101,555, but 30 years later, at the mine's peak, annual production would hit 90 times that amount.

Geologist Shirley Cragg came to the Porcupine and bought two veteran's lots near the Dome and 8 acres by Pearl Lake. He was acting for Fred Schumacher, and the purchase was a wise one, for the ground separated the Hollinger and McIntyre mines, while the land to the east would repay his investment later. Ohio-based Schumacher was wealthy from his patent medicine business long before he came to the Porcupine. He had read of the new camp and decided to invest. At the time, the community was known as Aura Lake, a reference to the gold beneath its surface, but it soon became known as Schumacher. Development of the mine of the same name was stalled by a squatter's shack located right on top of the proposed shaft. Schumacher could have just moved the family off, but instead he purchased the house.

One small immigrant group new to the mining camp were the Chinese. Harsh immigration laws hindered their settlement. These hardworking people found a niche outside of mining, for they were discriminated against by both the mines and the new union movement. The Chinese founded a service industry, opening restaurants and laundries.

One white worker raised her status. Clayton Ostrosser's wife made $400 annually as a teacher, but worked under poor conditions, with few supplies and no blackboard. Her lot improved dramatically when she was hired by the Hollinger manager to teach children resident on the property.

Early McIntyre Mine directors came north to survey the gold property.

- John Kirwan, Timmins Museum

One year after the great fire, excursion passengers enjoyed an outing at South Porcupine. - Timmins Museum

The first school at Golden City was rather spartan. - OA S15940

Gold samples were ever the topic of conversation in Porcupine.
- OA S 13439

Leo Mascioli moved to Timmins when the Cobalt camp started to slow down. His Italian countrymen came to Canada for a better life, but many were exploited due to lack of knowledge of English and, at first, their rights. Mascioli found he could make a better living than that made during his initial start as labourer and then foreman at the Hollinger. He began providing Italian labour to the mines and railway. He financed the men's passage from the old country in many cases, and they worked for him until their debt was paid. Later, in some instances, he even used his newcomers as strikebreakers.

Labour unrest swept much of the country in 1912, and the Porcupine was not left out. The advent of the railway had seen a drop in the cost of supplies, thus a cheaper cost of living. The mines attempted to cut wages and this focused the miners' grievances. The Porcupine Miners' Union was an affiliate of the Western Federation of Miners, linked with the Inter-national Workers of the World, known in some circles as the Wobblies. A strike from November until June 1913 shut down much of the camp. Demands were for improved bunkhouse conditions, safety rules, an eight-hour day and 50 cents a day increase in pay. The mines countered with trainloads of strikebreakers. Armed guards such as the American Theil Agency, hired by the Hollinger, aggravated the situation, and there were several violent episodes. Eventually a special squad of provincial police were called in to keep order. The strike was finally defeated and the miners gained little more than they had before. Miners who had not struck were given bonus pay, but this later became widespread. Gradually the big mines offered rental housing for families, and many of the ethnic workers bought lots and built their own homes. The strike was one of many that would plague the industry as miners sought improved wages and benefits.

The first strike in the camp, called by the Western Federation of Miners, lasted through the winter of 1912 and there were several scenes of violence.

- Timmins Museum

The hotel was not a palace but it served in the early days of Timmins.
- John Kirwan, Timmins Museum

CHAPTER 7

Quiet Years

After the fire, rebuilding and a strike which slowed the camp, the rest of the decade was one of steady growth. A new mine started up just east of the McIntyre. Known variously as the Coniaurus or Carium, it was a respectable producer for 48 years. Over at the Dome, Ambrose Monell replaced Edwards as president.

In town, Sam Bucovetsky built what became known as The Working Man's Store, the start of a northern retail chain. There was a flood around Porcupine Lake in 1913, the first of several before a flood-control system was set up many years later. More houses and stores were built than were occupied, but the town foresaw the need for increased fire protection and purchased a fire wagon – though the budget did not provide funds to obtain horses to pull it. Those citizens with delivery teams were expected to do their civic duty in the event of fire. At the sound of the alarm, teams raced to the fire hall. The first one to get there, hook up to the wagon and pull away received a $5 reward, thus adding to the usual excitement of a fire.

In planning the new community, the Hollinger management provided a building on the hill between the lake and the mine to serve as a church, with a residence close by. The building on the hill was much superior to Tom King's amusement place on Pine Street, which had been used for the first Protestant services and Sunday school. Most people thought a combination bar, billiard parlour and dance hall unsuitable for church functions. Percy Robbins, the Hollinger manager, finally gave the community church to the Anglicans. At the time, there was a family living in the rectory and the incoming minister had to wait for them to leave. Furnishings and hymnals were provided through donations and fundraising. (Single miners were glad to pay for home baking.) A black-face group, the Yama Yama Minstrels, raised money for new pews. The Roman Catholics also had become well established, and energetic and popular Father Theriault founded St. Anthony's Church.

Leo Mascioli was doing well enough in 1914 to build his first Empire Theatre. Another commercial establishment was Hamilton's Livery and Barn, which advertised "free rigs – tomorrow." Men could also get a haircut there while waiting for a ride. The Hollinger paid its first dividends in 1914 and announced reserves estimated at a minimum of $13 million, with mill output raised to 800 tons a day. Mine work was hard. Three-hundred-pound piston-type drills were used, and two men were required to get them in position. To cool the drills, water was ladled down the drill holes.

War came in 1914 and Canada went off the gold standard. Popular economic thought was that the standard restrained the expansion of credit, but it also had the effect of linking national economies. The railway began to carry young men away to serve their country. Governor General Earl Grey visited and observed the new town with its electric lights. Men lined up at the recruiting office for "the Forestry Draft." As with other centres, the gold camp saw some German activists shipped away for internment. Over 200 Serbians, Montenegrins and Italians joined up to serve their adopted country.

Racial discrimination surfaced in 1915. At a Board of Trade meeting, the president asked if it were lawful to employ white girls in Chinese restaurants. He was assured that this was only possible if there was an open dining room. The Sanitary Steam Laundry went one step further. Its advertisement read, "Is the Chinaman of Today to be Canadian Tomorrow? Let's Hope Not." Area residents were asked to patronize the establishment because all its employees were white. Citizens were reminded that if they used a Chinese business, they were contributing to the estimated $500 it cost to bring over another Chinese immigrant.

A tentative step was made toward mine safety when new regulations were instated concerning cage doors. Now cages had to be closed at least 5 feet above the floor. The newly published *Northern Miner* lauded this move, recalling how many miners had been caught in cage openings or thrown from them due to lack of support. It was estimated that 150 men still lived in area bunkhouses while the miners continued to support town development. The new Timmins waterworks issued $95,000 worth of debentures and the Hollinger took the lot. Such assistance was most helpful. The growing town still had a police force consisting of only a chief and one constable. Justices of the peace were paid on a fee-for-service basis, the chief worked days, and the night constable also doubled as sanitary inspector. The only paid fire department official was a fire inspector, who received $25 monthly.

The Aumont family all worked together in the bush around the Porcupine in 1914-5.

- John Kirwan, Timmins Museum

The fire department had to wait for volunteers to loan their horses.

- Bert Schaffer

W.M. Pritchard on his Pierce Arrow motorbike outside the Goldfields Hotel 1916.

- John Kirwan, Timmins Museum

Grocery and other deliveries came in this elegant wagon.

- John Kirwan,
Timmins Museum

HOLLINGER MINE'S NEW OFFICE, TIMMINS, ONT.

The mine is closed but the buildings survive.
- Author collection

In this 1918 Tisdale police picture, there is an OPP officer top right, liquor inspector middle second left, next to famed northern magistrate Siegfried Atkinson. Man in middle front is Hollinger security.
- Timmins police

The great fire which swept through Cochrane and Matheson in 1916 still holds the record for the number of people killed in Canada in a forest fire. The Porcupine was largely spared from the force of the killer fire, but it was a signal for Timmins to consider a full-time fire department. In a flurry of activity, a new fire hall was built on the corner of Cedar Street and Fourth Avenue. A fire wagon was purchased and a street alarm system installed. There were many more buildings to protect now.

The Finns were the largest ethnic group in the camp, and they built community halls. The halls were intensely political in association, with the Harmony Hall serving the right-wing group and the Finn Hall catering to left-wingers, who became allied with the Ukrainians in the union movement. The Jewish community was also strong enough to build a synagogue, located where Timmins Transit now stands.

The McIntyre was strengthened when it consolidated with the Jupiter and McIntyre Extension mines. The Dome was enlarged with the addition of the Dome Extension. The property had grown to 440 acres, and though open pits were still in use, the mine hedged its bets by continuing underground operations. The war hampered production by creating manpower shortages. In common with the other mines, the Hollinger found the new Workmen's Compensation Act of 1916 costly, but at least some provision was made for injured workers. The mine was the first in the camp to place electric locomotives underground, and they paid for

themselves in six months due to savings in manual tramming of ore. Children of those who lived in Fred Schumacher's adopted town had reason to thank the mine owner. From 1916 forward he provided money to obtain Christmas gifts for all those attending public school.

The labour situation in the mines became more serious, and the Dome ceased production in 1917 for the duration of the unrest. The respite was used for necessary underground development. The other mines just limped along. The McIntyre had good news with the declaration of its first dividend. Sir Henry Pellatt of Casa Loma fame joined the company as a director. He had been active in the Cobalt camp.

Timmins' population stood at 3,229 in 1917. A popular complaint of the time was the condition of roads between the communities. A mining inspector said of such highways, "They were not merely bad, they were damn bad." Better news came on the municipal front. Police officers came and went, probably due to better wages in mining, but the fire department was finally made full-time. A full-time chief, who also doubled as truant officer, received $100 a month and was supported by three paid firemen and 20 volunteers. Chief Alex Borland served until he retired in 1943 at the age of 77. He supervised the erection of a water tower and a 60-foot hose tower, which sported the big 9 o'clock curfew bell. The town purchased its own team of horses. The firemen were at the station 21 hours a day, with three one-hour breaks for meals at home.

Firemen's races were well attended. Returned soldiers watch at the corner of Pine and Second by the Friedman building, July 1, 1918.
- R. Ste. Pierre.

Ukrainian Social Democratic Party Drama Guild suit up for a play, 1919.
- Ukrainian Museum

The firemen were thankful that the severe March snowstorm which isolated the town for a week was not accompanied by a fire.

The Schumacher Mine closed in 1918 due to scarcity of labour. During its years of operation it had mined 27,182 ounces of gold and 4,195 ounces of silver. With his usual patience, Schumacher held on to the property until a good offer came along. The Dome continued its development work, and Jules Bache took over the mine and ran it until 1942. As soon as the war was over, the Hollinger built many new houses for miners and other staff. Its 2,600 shareholders were well pleased with progress and administration. A "Spanish flu" epidemic took several lives and strained health services in the Porcupine. The police chief was provided with a telephone and the authority to deputize special constables when required. Some members of the Chinese community attracted unwanted attention from the police for gambling and opium-smoking. There were frequent raids on Chinese establishments. The negative publicity was unfortunate, for most members of the Chinese community were industrious, model citizens.

The former West Dome Mine, where Bob Weiss and the others died, was incorporated with further claims in 1919 and became a big, new mine, the Paymaster. Over at Hollinger the new houses went for a rent of $18 a month, but the flat roofs were a poor design feature for the North Country and had to be converted to peaks. The Winnipeg General Strike focused attention on labour organization, but in the Porcupine, the mines, union, council and the Board of Trade actually got together to discuss the high cost of living. The mines helped by opening stores in Timmins and Porcupine, and selling goods at 15 percent less than prevailing prices. The policy was abandoned as the economy improved. The radical World Federation of Miners lost support in the North and the "One Big Union" took over. Its popularity was short-lived, and soon the dominant bargaining agent became the International Union of Mine, Mill and Smelter Workers.

Benny Hollinger was glad he had helped another as the decade came to a close. In various speculative ventures, he had gradually lost the money he had received for his staking of the Hollinger. He gave his name to a mine at Boston Creek, the Barry Hollinger, but received little from that gamble. Barney McEnany by contrast had done well from the claim Hollinger and Gillies had staked for him. He realized half a million dollars for what became the Porcupine Crown and had a one-sixth interest in it for a while. Now he came forward and bought Benny a home in Pembroke. A photograph taken of Benny Hollinger in 1919 shows the still youthful face of a man who looked too cultured to have ever endured the rough-and-ready life of a prospector. Benny never worked in the bush again and died of a heart attack at an early age.

Black face minstrel shows were popular in the Porcupine.   - John Kirwan, Timmins Museum

When the Prince of Wales toured the north in 1919, a loyal band was at the station waiting to greet him.
- John Kirwan, Timmins Museum

Regulation of blasting is a little more stringent today than it was in the early gold camp.   - Bob Atkinson collection

A gold pour at the Hollinger in the early days was marked by lack of safety equipment and security.   - OA S 15925

Once electric locomotives were introduced at the Hollinger, they soon paid for themselves over manual tramming. Left is Mr. Matimish, right is unknown.

CHAPTER 8

Progress and Disaster

After the post-war slump the Porcupine rallied to expand both the mines and the communities. New immigrants, often Italians and Russians, shovelled and performed most unskilled-labour jobs. Drillers were usually Finns, Swedes, Austrians or Poles. Tradesmen were generally from the British Isles or born Canadian, while engineering positions were primarily held by Canadians. The labour movement was not very active in the early twenties. The Cobalt strike of 1919 had not brought increased benefits to the mining camps, and union organizers felt the mining companies were too strong for strike activity to succeed.

Families like to be settled, and the mines provided more than just an hourly wage. All the large mines had townsites and offered houses at low rents. They backed the hospitals and had grocery stores which gave credit. Inexpensive recreational equipment was provided so that there was always some form of activity to occupy spare time. There was some political organization, mainly among ethnic groups. The Ukrainians built their Labour-Farmer Temple. Many were socialist and felt that, moving from the old country to the new, they had exchanged one set of inequities for another. Many sent money home to relatives working in mines in the Ukraine. They were supporters of the area Co-operative movement, which operated a bakery and even a boarding house. They also organized a huge literacy campaign in all the northern towns.

The McIntyre was well established by the early twenties, and in 1924, with the addition of the Plenaurum and Platt Vet properties, it had a total of 626 acres. The original hard-luck mine of the three great properties of the Porcupine was now in a position to advance Conn Smythe much of the money he needed to build the Maple Leaf Gardens. Through 1923 the Dome paid a total of $2.50 in dividends. Fred Schumacher's patience paid off when he sold his mine and 150-ton mill to the Hollinger for $1,733,333. Years earlier, he had been offered $75,000 for his Vet lots near the Dome, but he knew the ground was rich and decided to pay taxes on it rather than sell. Schumacher was more interested in real estate and finance than in mining. Mining was just a means of increasing his net.

Local men remembered getting hired at the Hollinger in the twenties. Mike Quinn was engaged just after the post-war slump, when there was a big crowd waiting at the gate. His job came because he had underground experience, always a premium in the mining game. Cliff McFadden breathed a sigh of relief when he was hired in 1923. He had never earned more than $70 a month before and work in the assay office was practically white collar.

In 1922 the camp swelled by 100 Cornishmen whom the Hollinger sponsored as experienced miners. Their entry to Canada was easier than that for the Chinese. From 1923 to 1947 the only Chinese who could enter Canada were those who had relatives in the country before 1923. To circumvent the Chinese Immigration Act, birth certificates were purchased from fellow countrymen who were going back to China to retire. These immigrants adopted the names on the papers they had purchased and became "paper sons." Many had to keep these names for a quarter of a century, until the act was repealed. The Italians were another group which helped each other. Some lived in "Little Italy" near the Dome, while others congregated at the south end of Timmins. Living conditions were hard at first. but the men had good jobs. Moneta became the name of their district, from the Italian word for coin.

Timmins' population had reached 4,545 by 1922. The town water supply was suffering from increased demands, and once again the Hollinger came to the rescue. The mine built a pump house and the town purchased its water from the mine. The arrangement continued until Timmins finally took over the system prior to the mine's closure. The Separate School Board built Holy Family School on Mountjoy in 1922. The Victorian Order of Nurses made their appearance in the district with their distinctive brown dresses, dark capes and hats. Police officers were paid $150 a month and spent much of their time enforcing the Ontario Temperance Act. Minutes from Police Commission deliberations show a decision to place a dummy policeman at the corner of Cedar and Fourth. Such dummies slowed motorists and required no pay. Money was not scarce. Pleasure-seekers could take a ride on the boats such as the *Minga*, the *Foche* and the *Haig*, which plied the Mattagami River. The Hollinger built the Timmins Golf Club. For many years, golfers had to play around raises that came to surface as well as open pits and other minor inconveniences.

Morin's store at the corner of Pine and Sixth held a good assortment of produce. - Bill Boychuk

The Goldfields was the most prominent hotel in Timmins for a long time. - OA 15380-75

The new Timmins Golf Course was overlooked by the Hollinger Mine.
— Joe Ferrari

Harry Peters photographed the camp from the beginning and the 1911 fire was one of his first jobs.
— John Kirwan, Timmins Museum

In early diamond drilling at the Hollinger Mine there was little in the way of protective gear for the miners.
— PA 17231

The Queen ruled the Winter carnival in 1924.   - John Kirwan, Timmins Museum

These horses were used for some work underground at the McIntyre Mine.
           - John Kirwan, Timmins Museum

Noah Timmins was not content with having made fortunes from two great mining camps. He noted the possibilities offered in a new Quebec camp. The president of Hollinger Consolidated Gold Mines called Sir Henry Thornton of the CNR and suggested that a line be constructed from the Quebec-Cochrane route to service Rouyn. Timmins joined the board of Noranda Mines in 1925 and advanced a huge sum for the time. "For the purpose of providing the necessary buildings, plant and machinery to fully equip the Company to carry on its operations in mining and smelting" the Hollinger put up $3 million. The loan was secured in ten-year bonds and no money was paid until Noranda had spent a million dollars.

The province bowed to pressure from all sides and formed the Provincial Air Service in 1924. The Porcupine fire and two other great fires, all within the space of 11 years, convinced Queen's Park that the public would not stand for continued loss of life and property. Timmins firemen had cause to rejoice as the town spent $12,000 on its first gas-powered fire truck and hose car. Horses were not phased out until 1934, but firefighters' hours were better, as the men now worked only seven 12-hour shifts a week. The police soon had their first car, a Studebaker Standard Six. Leo Mascioli's fortunes continued to expand as he built the grand Empire Hotel and also the Goldfields Theatre.

The prospectors returned to the Porcupine in 1926. Copper had been found in the Rouyn area and there were similarities in the ground. Gold had been found in small quantities near Kamiskotia Lake west of Timmins. When George Jamieson found five percent copper-zinc ore, another staking rush was on. Rumour had it that the place would be a second Noranda after nearly 5,000 claims – almost 200,000 acres – were taken up in the hot new area. But the base-metal market began to slip while gold firmed. Claims lapsed for lack of interest, and 40 years would go by before the copper was mined.

More alarming news came from the Department of Health. A spot check of 235 Porcupine miners showed heavy incidence of silicosis, in some cases allied with tuberculosis. In 1926 the whole camp was surveyed for the condition and 94 cases were compensated under the Workmen's Compensation Act. The silica content of the ore bodies in the camp was high, 40 percent, compared to less than a quarter of that in the nickel mines of Sudbury. Particles of silica inhaled over long periods scarred workers' lungs and impaired their function. The problem was one which the mines could not ignore.

In 1926 the Co-operative of New Ontario started its half-century run on the Timmins business scene. From a modest beginning with a capital of $4,000, it offered members lower prices and a say in company operation. The organization grew to include stores in six communities, plus boarding houses, a bakery and a dairy. The Co-operative aided community events and was supported by all groups in the communities.

The Buffalo Ankerite Mine opened in 1926 and was a steady producer for 30 years. The next year the McIntyre completed its great number 11 headframe, which can still be seen across Pearl Lake. The six-compartment excavation was 4,250 feet deep and 160,000 tons of rock were removed in its construction, as well as 40,000 tons of water. The project included 240,000 pounds of powder to blast the rock and 2,256,000 feet of Douglas fir to timber the shaft. As the "Mac" plunged deep into the ground, the Hollinger looked skyward and completed a 3½-mile tramway. For several years the slimes or tailings had been hauled away to the McKay claims, and now sand was brought by the tramway for backfill. Every 18 seconds a bucket carrying 1,800 pounds of sand crossed Highway 101 near the company offices, to a total of three-quarters of a million tons of fill annually.

The Hollinger once more supported the community, this time by building an 80-bed hospital on the site of the former one. In sports, a Scottish Football Association team played "Pick of the North" in soccer at the Timmins Athletic Grounds. Canadian players came from the long-time rival mines, the Hollinger and the Lakeshore of Kirkland Lake. But the big event in 1927 was the opening of a highway link between Timmins and Toronto. There was a great cavalcade of autos from northern points to celebrate a way out on a road which was only paved on the southern portions. One roadster was called the South Porcupine Wild Cat.

High-grading plagues all precious-metals camps. Walter Wilson was one of those who managed to lay hands on high-grade ore that never found its way to the Canadian Mint. In 1927 Robert Allen,, a detective for the Porcupine mines, worked on the theft case. Wilson had a good racket. Getting the stuff was not difficult but selling it presented problems. He arranged this by having identification referring to himself as part of the Wilson Mining Company. Detective Allen dogged his quarry for six months, and when Wilson was running short of funds, he arranged to sell gold to a Montreal jeweller and his wife. Allen moved in after 14 pounds of high-grade had changed hands for $2,000. The detective had arranged for police support, and he arrested Wilson and his buyers at the Porquis Junction station. The jeweller received a few months jail, as he admitted that the transaction had taken place. Wilson, however, beat the charge because he did not have all the money on his person. An appeal by the Crown landed him with two years. But on release, he returned to the old gold game. Wilson was the builder-operator of a famed dancing spot on the Mattagami River, the Pavilion, or more popularly, the "Pav." The building was wrecked in recent times. Not far away, a house was also torn down. People said they had never seen a place demolished so quickly –

If these rough-poured bricks contemplated by the worker with the chipped cup were worth $113,000 in 1920 on $20 gold, they would be valued at $2,683,750 with the price at $475 Canadian an ounce in 1990.
- Fred Rogers collection

George Zolob was a hero in the 1928 Hollinger fire.   - Ukrainian Museum

The Dome had made much progress by the mid twenties.
- Timmins Museum

many figured the workers had found squirrelled-away high-grade in the walls.

Noah Timmins' gamble with Noranda Mines paid off in 1928. The rich new mine repaid the Hollinger loan, principal and interest, in three years. Timmins himself received Noranda shares in exchange for options held in related Quebec mines, and the Hollinger gained the right to representation on the Noranda board for many years.

While the industry was achieving another health milestone in the requirement of annual chest x-rays for all miners, a tragedy struck one of the Timmins mines, one which would have far-reaching effects on Ontario mining.

The Hollinger was the largest gold mine in the British Empire. The mine was a good corporate citizen in the community and paid annual dividends of more than $5 million. All this was forgotten on February 10, 1928, when smoke began to curl up from its main shaft house. At first no one could understand how fire could take place in a hard-rock mine. Hundreds of miners escaped to surface, but the news soon spread that others had been trapped on the 550-foot level. The Hollinger had its own safety inspector, in addition to the government official, but he had not visited all of the more than 100 miles of underground workings. (The mine was so big that by the sixties it would have almost six times that tunnel mileage.) Mined-out stopes were not backfilled with waste rock, but one on the 550-foot level had been filled over the years with mining debris such as powder boxes, sawdust and wooden crates. The fire likely started by spontaneous combustion.

There were 920 men underground on the day of the fire, and even as they fought their way to shafts and manways leading to surface, outside help was on the way. A special train came from Toronto with fire department rescue experts, as well as technicians from Consumers' Gas and much equipment. All T&NO signals were opened and the train made the run in 14 hours, a record five hours less than the regular timetable ran. At the time, the industry was not equipped by regulation or design to fight a major underground fire. Another appeal was made to the U.S. Department of Mines, and a relief train was sent from Pennsylvania with rescue personnel experienced in coal-mine fires. The train went flat out and did the trip in 22 hours. Though the expertise offered was invaluable, 39 men died.

There were many acts of heroism in the hours and days that followed. Cage-tender Pete Benki stayed at his post until all the men were brought up from underground. Mine captain George Pond dragged Ira Graham to safety but fell on his carbide lamp and was burned in the process. Ossie Martin escaped but waited on surface for his twin brother. His sibling was finally brought to surface and Ossie took him home, dead. Two men

particularly stand out as heroes in the Hollinger fire. They were Fred Jackson and George Zolob.

Timberman Jackson's first reaction when he saw the smoke was that some of the muckers (underground labourers) had started a fire to keep warm, despite the fact it was a violation of mine regulations. He soon realized that the fire's scope was way beyond this possibility. Jackson was a member of the St. John Ambulance Corps and had some emergency training. George Zolob was one of the others on the 550-foot level. He had served in the Bulgarian army before coming to Canada and had been through wartime gas attacks. Independently Jackson and Zolob worked their way to the 675-foot level, with Jackson dragging an unconscious man part of the way.

They met up with 12 men who were trapped there. Both men realized help would be on the way. They broke an air line and played it on the rock wall to keep back the worst of the fumes. Jackson used artificial respiration on men overcome by smoke, while Zolob saw that the water and the little tea they had were shared. In the hours that followed they made string earplugs for relief from the noise of broken air lines. Shirts were torn to provide face masks, but the men became very cold and the lamps began to give out. At this point Jackson and Zolob decided to go for help. They stumbled, dashed and sometimes crawled through smoke-filled areas to reach the number 11 shaft. As they rang for the cage, the rescue party was on its way. Both Jackson and Zolob were near collapse from exhaustion but were able to give the location of the men they had left and others they had met along the way. Twelve men were saved by their efforts.

Over the next few days 39 men were brought up who had not escaped the smoke and carbon monoxide. The *Porcupine Advance* put out a special free issue giving the list of the dead, funeral arrangements and other details, saying it had taken the step because so many involved were "personal friends of this newspaper." Money for relief poured in from northern mining camps and donors in the south. Some victims were buried in Timmins or other parts of the country, while several others were interred in a common grave strewn with evergreens. As people like Dolphis Charboneau went underground with gas masks to hose down drifts, blowers pushed out noxious fumes. A coroner's jury viewed the work places and where the fire started. The Hollinger advanced all bereaved families $200 for expenses until Workmen's Compensation took over.

Out of suffering often comes some good. An Ontario inquiry into the worst disaster in its mining history laid no blame for the fire, saying that the best regulations are ineffective if some are ignored. The coroner's jury went further, declaring the mine management to be negligent. Among the inquiry's recommendations was one that mine rescue stations be set up in major mining camps. Such centres would be operated by the

Flooding in the Porcupine in 1928.

- Mattagami Conservation Authority

Department of Mines, with equipment for all possible emergencies. The safety officer in charge would also conduct training in area mines on a regular basis. This was acted on at once, and in 1929 Timmins received the first mine rescue station in the province.

The Ontario Mines Association contributed to the rescue stations via levies under Workmen's Compensation. A new group, which grew into the present Mines Accident Prevention Association of Ontario, promoted mine safety through education programs. Fred Jackson was unable to resume work for months due to the severe strain he had suffered in the rescue attempt. He rose in the Order of St. John and received its Life Saving Medal. George Zolob gained no recognition other than the respect of his community, and he went back to underground mining. The valuable lessons learned at the Hollinger fire and the official emphasis on accident prevention were to stand the Porcupine in good stead 37 years later, when another great mine fire struck the McIntyre Mine.

There was a heavy flood at Porcupine Lake in 1929, although it would take ten years before an efficient outlet was constructed to prevent further flooding. McIntyre manager Dick Ennis made a speech in which he remarked that the combined payroll of the Porcupine mines was three-quarters of a million dollars a month. At his own mine, Sandy McIntyre was awarded a life pension for the use of his name. (It was a good job that the pension came, as money never stuck in his pockets for long.) The camp could afford to be expansive in the year that closed the decade, for 176,626 ounces of gold and 932,732 ounces of silver were produced. A popular if irreverent saying of the time was that children prayed, "God bless Mummy, God bless Daddy, and God bless the Dome." That object of praise had its share of troubles. Its mill was destroyed by fire, but it unexpectedly reaped a bonanza from the misfortune. When the ashes were treated and floors scraped ready for rebuilding, $500,000 worth of gold bullion was recovered.

These men examine a vein in quartz at the 700 foot level of the Coniaurum Mine.
 - PA 17521

The filter press in the Coniaurum Mine in 1929 is now gone along with the mine. - PA 14310

The number 11 shaft house and waste ore bins, McIntyre Mine 1929.

The Dome mine with South Porcupine in the top background 1935.

CHAPTER 9

Depression and Boom

There was work in the neighbouring mining towns of Kirkland Lake and Timmins despite the fact that unemployment was high in the rest of Canada during the lost, depressed decade of the 1930s. While Timmins had its share of misfortunes and those without work, the gold town was not hit as hard as many other centres.

Timmins' population had grown to 13,007, and some could afford the luxury of a telephone. The directory was a slim volume which covered most centres in the Northeast, including Rouyn. Subscribers were advised that children and servants should not be allowed to listen in on a party line. In an arrangement which would not be permitted today, the telephone service was operated by the Northern Ontario Light and Power Company. The dual utility charged up to 10 cents per kilowatt hour and a rate of 3 cents for cooking.

The mines became more safety conscious after the Hollinger fire, and one development was improved rock bolting (as one miner put it, a process not unlike placing a toothpick in a club sandwich). Unions made little progress. The Workers' Unity League, through its affiliate, the Mine Workers' Union, organized miners in Timmins but made few gains. Pay was around $4.25 a day underground. Cliff McFadden saw as many as 500 samples a day in the Hollinger assay office. The place was busy and not at all similar to the white-collar work he had envisioned, but it was a job. There was still disposable income in the gold camp. The Italian community built their own church, and it was funded in part by bingoes.

Clary Dixon, the man in the canoe with Middleton on the day they heard Benny Hollinger's whoop of excitement, talked in the early thirties about his experiences. The youngest of the Porcupine stakers, he took less cash but was more prudent with it. His money purchased 2,000 Hollinger shares, which gave him a good income. He said, "I bought some Dome shares at fifty cents and sold them at three dollars to pay for a couple of years at university. You could say it was a rather expensive education because Dome kept going until in my time it reached forty dollars and even more. None of us, not even Noah Timmins, realized how important the camp was going to be, so we took the cash and let the credit go. The people who came later, when we made things easy, made the big money. But I'm afraid that's the way it will always be."

In the midst of the hard-luck stories of the early thirties, Fred Schumacher actually made money by inaction. He visited the Porcupine frequently but resided in Columbus, Ohio, where he built a great mansion and filled it with European art treasures. Shortly after he came into possession of the veteran lots near the Dome, he was offered $75,000 for them. Schumacher was in no hurry to sell, and he countered with a deal of double that price. The Dome ignored the offer and the matter remained in abeyance for 20 years. In 1931 the Dome was prospering and attempted to expand. The patient financier received a bid but repeated that $150,000 was still his price. He remarked that if his figure was not accepted, the next one would be $300,000. The Dome president rejected the deal.

Another wealthy man's generosity enriched the people in Ontario in 1931. David Dunlap, one of Noah Timmins' principal partners, first in Cobalt and later in the Hollinger, left money in his will for the David Dunlap Observatory north of Toronto. Dunlap once remarked that the Timmins brothers were a model of propriety in business matters: "In all our dealings there was never any written agreement between us. None was ever necessary."

The *Porcupine Advance* rebuked the Cochrane *Northland Post* for what it felt was a soft attitude on communism. In the column "Gravel, Sand and Placer," it reminded the rival paper that the communists were a menace to "the loyal Britisher and loyal foreigner" alike. Although Canadian communists were active during the Depression, they were generally driven out of the mining camps by the citizenry. Communists did get a hold in the Co-op movement simply due to member apathy. Thus Timmins found itself with two such stores. There was the red Workers' Co-op and the Consumers' Co-op.

Timmins people could now listen to a new radio station in North Bay but had difficulty with reception. The poor sound quality was easy to understand; owner Roy Thomson's first station was put together with second-hand and junk equipment.

Tough times saw no end to high-grading. Over $3,000 in gold was recovered from a store in the Moneta. Not all such theft was well organized or in such big volume. During night shift at the Hollinger, miners

The Northern Lights band played at the opening of Roy Thomson's CKGB *in 1933.*

- John Kirwan, Timmins Museum

At some long-forgotten parade, South Porcupine firemen honoured the British Empire.   - Draper photo

ХАЙ ЖИВЕ І МІЦНІЄ ЖІНОЧА СЕКЦІЯ ТУРФДІМ В 15 РІЧЧЯ СВОГО ІСНУВАННЯ.

The Embroidery Club at the Ukrainian Labour Temple 1934.
                    - Ukrainian Museum

The McIntyre Mine had its own ball field.
                                    - PA 17692

In the thirties the lumber industry workers made a lot less than miners.   - Timmins police

walked to surface in one of the raises that came up on the golf course. A chunk of ore could be thrown over the fence and picked up at leisure after the shift.

Between 1900 and 1931 the clay belt in the Cochrane District, in which the Porcupine stands, experienced the fastest growth in Northern Ontario. Those who came to farm were influenced to do so by Ontario government departments as well as by the T&NO Railway. Pamphlets, articles, exhibits and lectures all extolled the virtues of the land, yet even as late as 1919 Ontario Premier Sir William Hearst bluntly described it as "the most barren and God-forsaken country in the whole northland." The promotional campaign was ridiculous, but many would-be pioneers believed it. The snow was said to be beneficial to the good life, and crops grown in the region were called superior. People came by the hundreds and settled. For most settlers it was a hard life. Young men wasted the best years of their lives working on undrained soils that required heavy machinery and extensive capital. Winter was underestimated. Provincial Premier Mitchell Hepburn was forced to admit that colonization had been a costly error. Even today there are many buildings in the Porcupine area where the land has been abandoned and fields have reverted back to the bush.

Art Humphreys stayed in lumbering. For some years he worked for the Double Diamond mill. The operation had a double-cut band saw with a gun-shot feed. One man set the log and another held it on hooks to go through the saw cut. Humphreys saved money to go in partnership with the A.E. Wicks Company. Its mill operated on the Mattagami River, and though the mill is long gone, the present fountain near the bridge stands on the foundation of the former Wicks mill. Life was hard and millworkers received much less than miners. Pay was from 17 to 22 cents an hour. The mills in the area joined in the Mattagami Booming Company, which ran logs down the river before the use of trucks in the forties.

The Dome mill was rebuilt in less than a year after its fire, and the McIntyre completed a 2,000-ton mill at the same time. The Hollinger was mining more economically using the slice-and-fill method rather than that of shrinkage stopes. By this means ore was removed as mined and not left until the area was cleaned out. Successful mines are often a result of consolidation. Like the Buffalo-Ankerite, the Paymaster Mine put two properties together to operate as a fair-sized producer. Old-timers recalled that one of the shafts was the site of the underground deaths during the 1911 fire. The Buffalo-Ankerite was incorporated in 1932 and held ground west of the Paymaster. As for the great Dome not far away, they kept finding good ore in the country rock. Below the Dome, in its Extension property, a rich ore body was located in 1933. The previous year, Porcupine gold mined in 12 months came to $22 million. Ontario produced three-quarters of all the gold mined in Canada and 96 percent

of that came from the Porcupine and Kirkland Lake camps. Good news was that the trading price for gold moved $1.28 an ounce to $21.95, the first significant hike in 20 years.

Timmins' population stood at 14,519 in 1932 and the community expanded even in depressed times. The Polish White Eagle Society built a hall, as did the Yugoslavs. Unfortunately, like many groups from middle European countries, the Balkan immigrants split into factions and two halls were soon necessary, one for the left-wing Yugoslavs and one for the Croatians, who were right-wing. At the same time, Leo Mascioli took a block of land between Pine and Cedar streets, where fire had levelled property, and there he built the Palace Theatre. And young newcomer Wilf Spooner chose a good town in which to start selling fire insurance.

Long-time union organizer Bob Miner estimated that in 1932, for all the number of mines operating, there were still hundreds of men outside the mine gates hoping to get a job. The bonus system was in effect in most places and pick-and-shovel work was better than mechanical methods adopted later, as a shovel did not stir up much dust. He knew miners were lucky, as their work was steady, not like at the pulp mills, where men were often laid off two or three times a year. One man told him that he felt miners would one day make a dollar an hour, and Miner thought the dreamer had been smoking opium.

In 1933 transmission lines were cut through the bush, ready for power which would come from the Abitibi Canyon plant. Forest workers struck for better wages and conditions, but these would not come until the Depression had waned. There may have been hard times, but there was enough money around for moonshine to be a profitable if illegal product. The papers were never short of reports of illicit stills and liquor seizures. There was a story of the arrest of women vagrants and an account of the burglary of the Empire Cigar Store. Socialites could attend a Tennis Dance at the Empire, and J.P. Bartleman was elected to council. The young man who survived the Porcupine fire had done very well for himself.

The annual *Gold in Canada* reminded readers in 1933 that gold was always the leading guarantor of monetary systems. Venture capitalists obviously thought so, for two new properties were quietly being assembled. The Porcupine Grande, Three Nations and La Palme ground had never yielded dividends for their owners as individual mines, but as one unit they showed great promise. Noranda Mines evidently agreed. The Quebec-based firm bought the new venture from its original developers and set about building the Pamour Mine. This was the year that Fred Schumacher once more had some fun with the Dome management. As underground workings approached his property, he responded to overtures from the president by saying that he had not changed his last price

Weighing a gold brick at the Hollinger Mine 1936, chief assayer Mr. Scott. — PA 17552

and if it was not accepted, the figure would double to $600,000. Strangely, the offer was declined.

A stout, ambitious salesman from North Bay had observed the City of Timmins and its commercial potential for some time. Roy Thomson had opened a radio station in the Gateway City on a shoestring and promises to pay creditors. He came to the Porcupine and met J.P. Bartleman. The tall, gaunt insurance salesman with the booming voice could see the need for a radio station in the gold camp. He leased Thomson space in a frame building on Spruce Street opposite a brothel and assorted bootleg joints. Leo Mascioli was not interested in backing Thomson's venture, but Roy sold him an icemaker for the Empire Hotel. The radio station was built from old equipment by Thomson's faithful underpaid engineer. The long-suffering technician was almost arrested for working without union employees, and Thomson had to agree to pay the prevailing rates. The station opened in December 1933 with a few records and a piano. One announcer recalled playing "In a Monastery Garden" five times the first day. To gain advertising sales, merchants Sam Bucovetsky and Sam Fishman were practically provoked into competition via the airwaves, then station revenue was assured as sales rates went up. Mascioli would not advertise, as the ice machine Thomson had sold him was faulty. Difficulties in meeting payroll for the fledgling station were such that the wily owner issued pay cheques on a North Bay bank because he knew they would take longer to clear. His radio and sales force cashed their cheques promptly, before they had a chance to bounce.

Bank failures in the United States meant good fortune for the Porcupine and other gold camps on January 31, 1934, when Roosevelt raised the price of gold to $35 an ounce. Work began on marginal properties and exploration was stimulated. The new Pamour Mine received its charter. Geologist Doug Wright began to look at the long-abandoned Preston East Dome property. As for Harry Preston, he still basked in the glory of having found the great Ida Maud vein at the Dome. Away in Montreal, Noah Timmins had not forgotten the Larose Mine of Cobalt, which had been the basis of the family fortune. He gave $15,000 to Fred Larose, the man who had sold his associates the silver property.

As the Porcupine echoed with optimistic mining talk, compensation costs for victims of silicosis soared. The search for a way to control the dust-created disease was spearheaded not by a doctor but by a metallurgist. James Denny headed the metallurgy lab at the McIntyre. In previous work at the Nipissing Mine in Cobalt, he had noticed that aluminum seemed to eliminate silica in silver separation. Mine manager Dick Ennis and owner J.P. Bickell supported his work in the laboratory, and the research was aided by a medical team from Sir Frederick Banting's medical research institute in Toronto. Over the years the joint efforts of

the research teams determined that if silica particles in the lungs could be rendered inactive or inert, then scarring of the lungs would not take place.

The Timmins merchants were a lively bunch and in the mid-30s they did their best to attract business. Sam Bucovetsky had had the *Timmins Press* print a special advertising issue based on his store. His motto was the same as that of the Prince of Wales, *Ich dien*, or "I serve." Henry Ostrosser worked in his father's menswear store. Improved gold prices perked up business, and instead of spending $12 for a good suit, some customers went for more expensive lines. Miners were making $4.25 a day in 1934 and paid $3.95 for a pair of shoes. Borsalino hats were popular and retailed for $7.95. A few customers were "kiters" who paid with dud cheques. At the Ostrosser's store such cheques were placed under glass on the counter. The practice discouraged cheats.

Drunk charges still rated front-page space in both newspapers. This contrasted with announcements that beer could once more be legally sold. In fact one establishment gave out free samples. The papers castigated the province about poor roads. One family came north with a truck from Toronto but found roads near Matheson practically impassable. Many thought relief work should repair the stretch between South Porcupine and Timmins because it was "a menace to life and property." There was a move to build a road from Timmins to Matachewan, but this is still just a bush track.

The city had police problems in 1934. One chief was unhappy with local provincial police members and tried unsuccessfully to have them replaced. As it happened, council fired him later in the year. By contrast they were pleased with the new fire chief, who received $165 a month plus free house and telephone. It was reported that "the stork outdistanced the Grim Reaper" with 45 births in one month and only 16 deaths. Finally, "Inky" Wood of Schumacher was said to be a sensational right-hander in the Northern Ontario baseball championships.

Councillor Bartleman was feuding with the *Porcupine Advance* and started a rival paper, *The Citizen*. He succeeded in antagonizing much of the electorate, so Roy Thomson offered to take the paper off his hands for $200 down and promissory notes of $200 a month for 28 months. Bartleman did not like the deal, especially since he still owed money on the printing press, but he succumbed to Thomson's suggestion that if he went bust, Bartleman would get the paper back. With his usual gall, Thomson bought newsprint from Iroquois Falls on credit, could not afford wire services, and persuaded the federal government that it was not a bad thing to own both a radio and newspaper in the same town. Then he studied American papers to see the ratio of news to advertisements. He competed with the *Porcupine Advance* for advertising revenue. He had not enough type to print more than eight pages, so

Walter Honer pours a gold bar in 1934 at the Dome. - Timmins Museum

Lawrence Hazard drove this team from Porcupine to Ottawa in 1939 to commemorate the royal tour.
- Draper photo

would often repeat stories if more sales space was needed. The new *Timmins Press* sported the slogan "If it will help the North, we are for it."

Timmins builders had a record year in 1935, with 427 permits issued for $391,023 worth of construction. Among the new buildings was Schumacher Public School. At that time the Board of Education operated a teacherage for 15 single women teachers. The police department received their first van. When one officer had difficulty getting a prisoner into the vehicle, a woman bystander rushed up and hit the offender on the nose. This gave the new van its second occupant.

The stability of $35 gold lasted for 37 years. A new federal regulation further stimulated the industry. Any new Canadian gold mine was exempted from income tax for the first three years of production. One result was the revival of a long-dormant property, the Preston East Dome. Geologist Doug Wright was convinced the old place would make a mine. He interested promoter Joe Hirshorn in the project, but Hirshorn was slow to make up his mind. They met and discussed the matter in the financier's New York skyscraper office. When Hirshorn still hesitated, the exasperated Wright threatened to throw him out of the window. This prompted a favourable decision, and when the ground was drilled, a substantial tonnage of gold was located. Financiers on Bay Street were lukewarm to the venture, so Hirshorn took the unusual step of floating a bond issue which guaranteed that the required $600,000 would be repaid in five years. His confidence was well founded, for the debt was paid off in four years.

The new Pamour Mine went into production in 1936, and with Noranda as the owner, the company found itself funded by the Timmins interests back in the Porcupine, where it had gained much of its start. The new mine revitalized the community of Porcupine; many of its miners chose to live there. Noranda put together the Poulet Vet and Porcupine Creek claims to form the Hallnor Mine, honouring the firm's assistant general manager, Oliver Hall. This followed shortly after with another mine, the Aunor.

In 1936 Fred Schumacher concluded the deal with the Dome that had first been suggested to him in 1912. The South Porcupine mining firm picked up the Foley-O'Brien claims at the same time, but they were a straight cash purchase, as compared to the protracted negotiations with Schumacher. The Dome received the ground for $1,125,000 plus 20,000 Dome shares which split later two for one. The mine paid for its half-hearted attempts to secure the property over the years. They would have been further ahead to have taken the price the financier first offered them. The story of how the "reluctant" vendor kept doubling his price when initial offers were not accepted went into the mining lexicon as "Schumachering." The Dome manager presented Schumacher with a rich gold ore specimen as a souvenir of the deal. He did not realize that

Schumacher had known for 24 years the potential of the property he had just sold.

Long-time Timmins Mayor Leo Del Villano met Noah Timmins in 1924, when Leo, then 11, was caddying on the Hollinger course. Leo later remarked, "He was just an ordinary guy and a prospector, which I could relate to." The "ordinary guy" died in Palm Beach, Florida, on January 23, 1936, at the age of 69. Timmins was the last of the five associates who developed the great Larose Mine in Cobalt, and he then went on to prove the Hollinger Consolidated. He had success in fields other than mining and was a director of 21 companies at the time of his death. The funeral took place at St. Leo's Church in Westmount, Quebec, and Timmins priests Fathers O'Gorman and Theriault officiated. T.A. Crerar, Federal Minister of Mines, gave the eulogy. Noah Timmins was always popular in the city Al Pare had named for him. He would have liked his obituary in the *Northern Miner*. "He was a builder and the country could do with more like him."

Timmins' son Jules took his place as president of the company. Jules had come up the hard way through operation of the big mine and had worked underground. Jules later founded the Iron Ore Company of Canada. Another son, Leo, took his father's former seat on the Noranda board. Even in the year its founder died, the Hollinger was taking to the surface thousands of tons of gold from the 800-foot level. (This ore was now profitable thanks to the rise in gold prices.) The great all-concrete headframe was completed in 1936 and ore came up it in counterbalanced 5-ton skips. The building still graces the Timmins skyline.

Thelma Barkwell came to the gold camp in 1936. At first the young nurse thought it was a rugged place, but she found a great social life and, like so many newcomers, she enjoyed dancing at the Pavilion on the Mattagami River. Timmins was a city with a housing shortage and newly announced federal loans for new home construction was welcomed. Friedman's offered school dresses for a dollar and work shirts for 50 cents. St. Anthony's Church burned and work started on a new place of worship. In the political arena, Thomson's newspaper and radio station endorsed Jimmy Bartleman for mayor. The *Press* feuded as much with Bartleman as any other municipal leader, but admired his dedication to the city. The media-sponsored candidate won, but the paper later reversed its decision to back him.

The City of Timmins marked its silver jubilee in 1937. There was much to celebrate. The country was coming out of the Depression and much had been accomplished in the Porcupine in a quarter century. The Lions Club arranged many special events. Denham and Harvey Greer made a trip to Ottawa by dog team. They had a grueling run but arrived to present Prime Minister Mackenzie King with an invitation to attend some of the Timmins festivities. The two modern-day coureurs de bois

STORY OF THE ROCHDALE PIONEERS
OF THE PORCUPINE CAMP

The Consumers Co-operative Society Ltd. founded in 1931 with 51 members and 1 store declared new principles of doing business.

NOT THIS
1 VOTE PER
SHARE OF
STOCK

1 VOTE PER PERSON

NOT THIS
PROFITS
TO
OWNERS

PROFITS TO MEMBERS

NOT THIS
AS HIGH
INTEREST
AS POSSIBLE

A FIXED RATE
OF INTEREST

—AND IN 1937 THERE WERE . . . .

650 MEMBERS
(Each figure represents 10 members)

Affiliated to the Co-operative Union of Canada

Fastest Growing Co-operative in Canada and the only genuine Consumers Co-Operative in the Porcupine Camp.

KEY TO SUCCESS
(1) Mutual Ownership Membership open to all consumers.
(2) Equal Rights One man, one vote.
(3) Democratic Control Unlike some co-operatives no group or political party control tolerated.
(4) Profits Returned to customers on basis of purchases.

$500,000.00 *Annual Sales*

$57,029.17 *Purchase Dividends Returned to Customers In less than 6 years*

DIRECTORS

N. Riihinen, Pres.	A. Heino, Sec.
P. Larmer	John Fell, Sr.
R. Todd	A. Long
Chas. Kanerva	M. Kautto
Kust. Leino	

C. M. Haapanen, Manager.

The CONSUMERS CO-OPERATIVE SOCIETY
LIMITED

Schumacher, Ont.	Timmins, Ont.	South Porcupine, Ont.
(Branch)	Main Store & Offices	(Branch)

The Co-op movement was strong in Timmins in 1937. - Author collection

Margaret Haines' one room school class near Shillington 1937.
- M. Haines

stood out on Parliament Hill in bright Hudson's Bay coats. The Prime Minister and his colleagues were in stark contrast in their dark business suits. The invitation almost guaranteed acceptance, for it was in the form of a gold plaque.

With parades and other celebrations, visitors could see activity throughout the city. Roughly one-third of the population was French Canadian, one-third Anglo Canadian (English, Scots, Welsh or Irish), and the balance of assorted ethnic origin. Many of the ethnic groups had their own churches and social halls. The Romanians built a church in the silver jubilee year. City officials estimated the value of buildings in the community at almost $15 million. South Porcupine completed a hospital on land donated by the Dome. The Riverside Dance Pavilion, the "Pav," became one of the main entertainment centres during the festivities. Walter Wilson's "Premier Dance Hall of Northern Ontario" was open all year. Advertisements advised smokers that during intermission they could chew Wrigley's gum between smokes, as it made the taste better. Inside they could dance to the Henry Kelnick Band, who dominated the local music scene for many years.

Outside the city one could visit the McIntyre's fine arena. Mine-owner J.P. Bickell had become the first president of the Maple Leaf Gardens (the outstanding-player trophy is named after him). Bickell wanted a comparable facility for his miners, and the new arena was one of the finest in Canada outside a major centre. The "Mac" was modelled after the Maple Leaf Gardens, and for a while, seating colours followed the same sequence. Later the Leafs would play exhibition games at the Mac, and Barbara Ann Scott used it while training for the world figure-skating championships. McIntyre miners received $13 a month in coupons good for arena services.

In that year of celebration, the bright future of the mines was most evident. Thirty-five million dollars worth of gold was produced by the Hollinger, McIntyre, Dome, Coniaurum, Buffalo Ankerite, Pamour, Paymaster and Vipond. The Delnite commenced production and operated for 27 years. One operation, the Tiny Hill Syndicate, announced that it was "probing rich spots in your North East corner," but no more was heard of that venture. No one remembers the outfits that missed the big strike. The Hollinger commenced operating an electric train on surface between its number 19 shaft house near Schumacher and the number 11 shaft. At 12 miles an hour, the trolley seated 50 men and beat the usual hike between work places, especially in miserable weather. The miners enjoyed the convenience of what they called "The Twentieth Century Limited" and, as the driver said, the outfit was a success because there was no competition.

Margaret Haine came to teach at S.S. #3 Currie in 1937. The one-room school was not far from Shillington. Perhaps ten percent of the teachers' college graduates that year were fortunate enough to get a teaching job, so the young teacher thought she was lucky at $700 per annum, or $67.90 a month once pension was deducted. She secured room and board in a log home not far from the school for $20 a month. Most of her pupils' parents were settlers under Hepburn's "Back to the Land" scheme. They knew little of farming but were rich in character. Margaret decorated her room with washed flour sacks and taught 29 students in grades one to ten by coal-oil lamp. The Imperial Daughters of the Empire gave her school a welcome collection of Canadian books. The school was only 38 miles from Margaret's home in Timmins, but she only went home twice a year, as the roads were bad and even a cutter or wagon trip to the station could become bogged down. The school no longer exists, but it lives in the hearts of those who went there.

Three new mines began producing gold in 1938. The Broulan Reef went on to operate for 27 years. The Preston East Dome was worked until 1968. Joe Hirshorn had used another innovative approach in financing the property. He had persuaded the contractors to build the mill and take bonds as part of the $700,000 payment. Once again he had the golden touch, and the bonds were redeemed within a year. The third mine was built in the shadow of the Hollinger, in the Moneta district of Timmins. The Moneta Mine was one of the richest in the camp, but the gold ore was mined out in six years.

City police now had Timmins Police Force painted on their vehicle doors. The mayor wanted the chief of police to investigate communist activity in the city, but the chief remonstrated that there was no problem with the reds because during times of prosperity citizens had no interest in communism. The fire department now had 12 paid employees and a brand-new pumper which could carry 1,000 gallons. On the labour front, the two rival Co-ops could not reconcile their differences and continued separate operation. Miners at the McIntyre and Buffalo Ankerite toyed with strike action, but the owners gave them an increase of 5 cents an hour and the idea was dropped.

As the decade came to an end Timmins had 25,119 citizens. The *Timmins Press* was unable to report on its own big story, as the press building burned. Roy Thomson had a higher credit rating than in the early days and was soon in operation again. The *North Bay Nugget* printed the paper for a month, then repaired presses rolled in Mascioli's Empire Theatre. Thomson negotiated a loan with J.P. Bickell and decided to put up a new building to house his paper and radio station CKGB. Jack Kent Cooke was his long-time ally, and he came to Timmins to boost advertising sales. Like Thomson, Cooke would make his own millions in years that followed.

Roy Thomson had every reason to be pleased with the progress he had made in Timmins. Leo Mascioli had come around and was now a big

Several workings are visible in this Hollinger #12 cut or 'glory hole' in 1936. - PA 17625

Shaft sinking at the Dome's 2,200 foot level in 1936. The bucket has been removed ready for blasting below. - PA 17559

In 1939 the headframes of the rich Moneta Mine were located right on the edge of downtown Timmins.   - John Kirwan, Timmins Museum

The shift is over. Miners wait for the cage at the 1800 level of the McIntyre Mine 1936.   - PA 17570

shareholder in the paper and radio station. For some years he had been associated with Jimmy Bartleman in business and politics. But Bartleman was always feuding with someone, and Mascioli became annoyed with CKGB Radio over coverage he received. The mayor tried to have council take over the station. He gained no support and the *Press* used words like "soviet" in its description of the embattled mayor. Even the paper's rival, the *Porcupine Advance*, sided with the *Press* in its fight against the mayor. The media backed taxi-owner Emile Brunette in the election and J.P. Bartleman lost his place as head of council.

Highway 11 was brought up to class-A standard by the close of 1939, and the distance to Toronto was reduced by 70 miles. Ben Bauman celebrated by cycling the 545 miles from Toronto to Timmins in 60 hours. He had trouble on the unpaved sections of the old Ferguson highway but was glad to be able to promote his community.

Timmins was unusual in another way. Just north of Porcupine Lake Mrs. J.A. Thoms held the distinction of being the only female mine operator in Ontario. She ran the Jodello and the MacGregor Porcupine properties just west of the High Pam Mine.

The Porcupine had come through the Great Depression and the camp seemed about to make more progress, but world war dampened that prevailing feeling of optimism.

Work clothes hanging in the McIntyre Mine 'dry' waiting for the next shift. - PA 17581

Heading for the punch house to clock off the job at the Hollinger 1936. Note the bucket line in the background. - PA 17577

Scaling down rock at the Hollinger, 1,700 foot level.

CHAPTER 10

War and After

The war slowed mining everywhere in Canada. Labour became scarce and marginal mines like the Vipond closed. An average of one-third of all miners in the camp went away to fight for their country. All mines contributed to the war effort. In addition to the production of gold, the Hollinger mined scheelite. A shortage of tungsten from overseas meant this host to that mineral was needed, as it was used in the manufacture of high-speed tool steel. The Dome made parts and equipment for pumps in cargo vessels. Some companies, like the Preston East Dome, matched employee donations to the Red Cross and war charities. There was work for all who sought it, and the mines paid a war bonus of 21 cents a shift. Citizens supported the RCAF Porcupine Squadron and HMCS *Timmins*.

This was a time when the Union Jack flew over all headframes as a symbol of liberty. It was also a period of suspicion and mistrust. Leo Mascioli and his brother were arrested and interned. At one point the busy builder had sent money to Italy and the Duce had given him a minor honour. Public figures came to his defence. Roy Thomson led the fight in the *Press*, Father Theriault took church action, and Jimmy Bartleman wrote pamphlets on the subject. Mascioli had been in the camp since 1911 and was a pillar of the community. The protests paid off, and the brothers were released towards the end of 1940. Italians held meetings to proclaim their loyalty to Canada, but many citizens of European descent were taken from important jobs in the mines and set to work with pick and shovel. As time went on, such unfair actions were reversed. One of the cruelest was against the Ukrainians. Their hall was confiscated and the adjacent park sold.

Even in wartime there was opportunity for a celebration. The art-deco-style Thomson building, constructed by Feldman Timber, opened in May 1940. The facility housed the newspaper and radio station CKGB. Thomson was happy, for he had finally bought out Bartleman's outstanding shares. The new radio station was equipped with a grand piano, pipe organ and "all fixtures necessary for the production of the finest radio." Dennis Braithwaite, who became a well-known Canadian writer, was an announcer at the time. He could be heard advertising tickets on Dalton's bus lines at eight for a dollar and ice cream for 15 cents a pint at the Top Hat Lunch. Liquor offences and bootlegging charges were frequent items in the news. Jack Kent Cooke sold advertising for both radio and newspaper, with the boast that he never took no for an answer.

A big forest fire, believed to be incendiary in origin, burned over 33,000 acres in 1941 and came within 6 miles of Timmins. Actions of the Mine Mill union fueled the big mines strike in Kirkland Lake. Huge sums were raised in the Porcupine for their fellow workers in the nearby gold town, but the strike was defeated and Kirkland Lake never again regained its output or manpower as a mining community. The McIntyre produced $9,433,891 in gold in 1941 and enjoyed its best recovery, despite labour and materials shortages. According to the fine copperplate script in the Buffalo Ankerite pay books, $1 was deducted from each cheque for medical benefits, there was bonus pay, and contributions were made to war loans. Every two weeks the superintendent took home $317.50, master mechanic $135, mechanic $109, and muckers earned $81.

Jeanne Larcher played the organ at CKGB. She also worked as pianist for the Cartier Theatre. Hers was a musical family (she noted that even her sewing machine was a Singer). One act which interested her was the Davis family dancers. The black trio of father, uncle and son tap-danced through a two-hour program. Jeanne was especially taken with the son, 16-year-old Sammy Davis Jr., who was pure magic on his feet. Times were hard for the trio, so the pianist invited the Davises home to have supper and meet her family. Travelling dancers did not make much money in wartime. They were hungry and had several helpings of her stew. Over the years Mrs. Larcher kept touch with Sammy and followed his path to stardom. She saved to see his performances in New York and Chicago and once visited him in his dressing room. She had played "Love, Your Magic Spell is Everywhere" for him during his visits, and later the entertainer recognized it in one of his albums. Right up to his death, Sammy Davis Jr. had a soft spot for Timmins and the lady who fed him stew when times were tough.

The population of Timmins stood at 28,274 in 1943, the year the Moneta Mine closed. It was a small property but very rich, averaging .47 ounces to the ton and having produced 150,000 ounces of gold, much of which was from veins that came in from the Hollinger at the 600-foot

Dome miners lunch at the 2,200 foot level close to the shaft.

level. Over at the Dome, president Jules Basche arranged for employees in the forces to receive $25 at Christmas. At home, the Mine Mill union won a fight to be certified at most of the mines, but under War Labour Relations Board regulations, no wage hikes were permissible anyway.

Sandy McIntyre, the man who gave his name to a great mine, lived in the public view for many years, but like so many prospectors, he had trouble holding on to the money he earned. At the time of his death in 1943, at the age of 74, he was dependent on the McIntyre pension for support. He had scored another big strike in Kirkland Lake, but had been unable to hold on to his good fortune in that camp too. Sandy yarned with Dick Ennis when he picked up his pension cheque, talking of his adventures in the Red Lake camp, but only once more made the national news, when he chatted in Gaelic with Governor General Lord Tweedsmuir, author John Buchan, when the dignitary passed through Swastika.

Tom Middleton bears comparison with Sandy McIntyre. Jack Miller paid him $28,000 for claims associated with the Hollinger. He too blew his money in a few short years and survived on a small pension.

Researchers Denny and Robson continued their work on silicosis at what became known as the McIntyre Research Foundation. Their observation that aluminum power could be used to prevent silica reaction in the lungs was confirmed by the Banting Institute. Mine-owner Jack Bickell enthusiastically supported their work. A clinic was established at St. Mary's Hospital in Timmins, and the success of the powder in treatment of silicosis sufferers persuaded the mine to administer the treatment to all employees. They made use of a system originally used to combat high-grading. Men up from a shift routinely put their lunch pails on a conveyor running through an inspection room while they changed and showered. In the new treatment process, the miners received the aluminum power in the "dry" while they were changing, then they boarded a moving platform running through a solarium, where ultraviolet lamps compensated them for sunshine they did not get underground. The procedure took 20 minutes. Within two years most gold mines in Ontario had followed the McIntyre's pioneering lead in silicosis treatment.

The city made progress even in wartime. By 1944 it had a public health unit. The fire department gained from innovation in smaller high-pressure lines, new chemicals to combat various types of fires, and fresh-air breathing apparatus. As the European war drew to a close, the Ukrainian people were compensated for confiscation of their property, at 14 cents on the dollar, but they had to pay for the utilities used in their building during the war period! The confiscated park was bought back for them by the city.

During the war years emphasis on mineral production was switched from precious metals to strategic materials. Viola MacMillan and her husband George had been prospectors in the Timmins area for many years and met with Mines Minister Tom Crerar to impress upon him how prospectors could help the war effort. Viola and George, long active in the Prospectors and Developers Association, offered to get 150 prospectors together if the province would offer courses in the recognition of strategic minerals. The first course was held and its success was such that several more followed in the North. The information gained by the prospectors resulted in an exploration boom which intensified after the war. As for Viola MacMillan, she had another part to play in Timmins a few years later.

The Hollinger was still the biggest gold mine in the camp. In 1945 it surpassed a total dividend payout of $125 million. The mine had 350 miles of underground railway. There were 36 locomotives, together capable of handling the nearly 1,500 ore cars that were maintained and operated by 165 men. The original principals had all passed on, but their sons were active on the board of directors. Jules, Noah Jr., D.M. Dunlap and Allen McMartin all carried on family involvement in the mine.

In the same year, Donald Tench was grateful he missed a bus. The Paymaster mine's late arrival at the mine meant he also missed his ride on the cage to the 1,500-foot level. On that February 2nd the hoist cable separated and the emergency "dogs" on the side of the cage failed to grab the timbers. All 16 miners on the cage plunged 2,500 feet straight down to their deaths. Don Tench worked to recover the dead, but his brush with disaster kept him off work for a few days afterwards. Then he went back to underground mining. It was the only job he knew.

After the war Timmins continued to develop as a community. The Porcupine Art Club started and had Group of Seven artist A.Y. Jackson as a guest speaker. Promising world-class figure-skater Barbara Ann Scott practised at the McIntyre Arena. The health unit had a public veterinary service. A private group of educators offered kindergarten to preschoolers. J.V. Bonhomme, a Timmins insurance agent, bought 480 acres south of the city, surveyed 50-foot-wide lots and started building houses for the post-war boom that was sure to follow. The new subdivision was called Melrose, for Bonhomme had financed his purchase from fees he received after selling the Melrose Theatre in North Bay.

Also in 1946, an inquiry was conducted into the operation of the Timmins police, then 23 in strength. There were allegations of poor conduct and theft of liquor from the police vault. The *Daily Press* gave the case several pages. Although no specific recommendations came out of the matter, the department was put on a more organized footing afterwards.

Ever an innovator, the Hollinger began offering evening classes related to its operation for employees who wished to better themselves. The courses became an annual event and were always well attended. The mine also started its own paper, the *Hollinger Miner*, a good example of a

The Hollinger Mine in 1939 had a fine park in front and neat plant.
- OA S1081

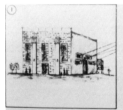

HOIST-HOUSE
ORE IS HOISTED FROM
3050 FOOT LEVEL IN 6.5
TON SKIPS AT SPEED OF
3000 FEET PER MINUTE

**SHAFT-HOUSE &
CRUSHING-PLANT**
MAXIMUM CRUSHING
RATE, TO 3/16 INCH MESH,
450 TONS PER HOUR

ORE STORAGE BIN
CAPACITY 10,000 TONS
CRUSHED ORE IS STORED
IN READINESS FOR THE
GRINDING OPERATION.

BALL MILL & CLASSIFIER
ORE IS GROUND TO A
VERY FINE SAND IN A
CYANIDE SOLUTION WHICH
DISSOLVES THE GOLD.

PULP & SOLUTION
PUMPS ARE USED TO
TRANSFER PULPS OR
SOLUTIONS AS REQUIRED IN
THE TREATMENT OF ORE.

CONCENTRATING TABLES
THE SULPHIDE MINERAL
PARTICLES ARE REMOVED
BY THE TABLES FOR
FINER GRINDING.

Schematic of parts of the Hollinger operation in 1947.
- John Kirwan, Timmins Museum

company paper, with a mix of mine operation news and stories of personnel. George White came back to the big mine after his war stint. He had not forgotten one of the first rules of underground survival: one never gets lost following running water, as it always leads to the shaft. George came on as an assistant mine captain. His pay was $1.09 an hour at a time when miners were making 57 cents. Generally, gold mining in Canada was at a low ebb. Production costs were rising and there was a fixed price for the end product.

A 1946 census revealed that Timmins' population was one-third French, 43.5-percent English, 5.1-percent Italian, 2.8-percent Finnish, 2.5-percent Ukrainian and 2.2-percent Polish. The year 1947 marked the end of restrictions on Chinese immigration. It was also the year Mike Ayoub embarked upon building the grocery empire which bore his name.

Fire is an ever-present bane of the North. In February 1947 the Timmins Arena went up in flames. The structure had been built in 1914 by the Hollinger Mine at a cost of $50,000, but it had long been super-ceded by the McIntyre Arena. In private hands since 1932, it was being used mainly for minor-league hockey games. Timmins police investigated and found five juveniles who admitted setting fire to one of the dressing rooms. The event drew attention to the curfew law. The big warning bell was still calling young people to go home after 9 o'clock, but youngsters were routinely playing hockey after that hour. The following year a 5,000-acre bush fire destroyed much property in the Kamiskotia area, including ski club buildings and a fire ranger's tower and cottage.

Compressed air was supplied to area mines from the plant on Gillies Lake in 1947. Gold bars valued at $50,000 regularly came out of the mines on the way to the Mint. The Hollinger noted in its company news-paper that it was currently producing one part gold to 116,667 parts waste rock. But the mines were expecting tougher times. The Pamour actually lost $24,000 due to fixed gold prices, but nonetheless paid a 7-cent-an-hour cost-of-living bonus. Across the country, people in the industry pressed the government for some relief while the price of gold stayed fixed. One person very active in this work in Timmins was J.V. Bonhomme. The international Monetary Fund had pegged the value of paper currency, and gold was moving away from use as a monetary metal as the U.S. dollar gained ground. The federal government finally recog-nized the problem and legislated the Emergency Gold Mining Assistance Act. This subsidized the mines for the difference between the price of gold and the cost of production. Without this step, many of the proper-ties would have closed.

The Timmins Royal Canadian Legion building added to the skyline in 1949 and a long-gone local businessman reached a milestone. Roy Thomson, the barber's son and school drop-out, had reached his goal of making his first million in business. Thomson was a late bloomer and had

many false starts; he was now 55, 25 years behind in his self-imposed financial schedule. The myopic, chubby hustler made his money by cutting costs at his papers and radio stations. He believed that "editorial content is the stuff that separates the ads."

In 1950 the Porcupine camp turned 40 years old. The *Daily Press* had a front-page slogan declaring that it covered "the Golden area of Northern Ontario." It was true for Timmins because the *Porcupine Advance* had ceased to publish. The firm had become a commercial printer instead. There was no room for two papers to be profitable in the Porcupine. The sole paper in the camp reported that South Porcupine native Pete Babando of the Detroit Red Wings won the Stanley Cup over Timmins native Alan Stanley of the New York Rangers. In mining news, labour was still in short supply and the mines were recruiting in the United Kingdom. Miners could buy safety glasses at cost, and if they worked for the Hollinger, they would receive a turkey from 10 tons of birds given to employees at Christmas. Art Humphreys, manager of the A.E. Wicks sawmill on the Mattagami, started selling sawdust and wood waste to the big mine. A new central steam plant used 17,000 tons of it in five months and saved a bundle over oil and other fuels.

Wilf Spooner became mayor of Timmins in 1951. He served the area well at various levels of politics and wound up as head of the Ontario Northland Railway board. Leo Mascioli died at the age of 75. The lad who at ten had posed as a man's son in Boston in order to satisfy immigration rules, had built the Empire hotel chain, garages, bowling alleys and several theatres. Mascioli had his detractors, but his work is still seen around Timmins.

Conrad Lavigne began with a grocery store, became a saloon-keeper, and in 1951 started the third entertainment outlet in Timmins, CFCL, a French-language radio station. Another long-time newsmaker died. Jack Bickell, McIntyre's president, had sponsored silicosis research. His will established a $13-million foundation with half of annual proceeds going to Toronto's Hospital for Sick Children, and the rest for other medical and educational projects.

Joe Ferrari had just entered grade school in the early fifties. He liked to visit the golf course by the Hollinger and peer through the big screen at the number-one hole at the miners down below. Over by the number-nine hole there was a raise where underground workers could walk to surface and eat their lunch. The mine had now introduced job evaluation. Rates of pay would be based on knowledge and skill rather than tradi-tional pay levels. Some miners were not happy with the new scheme and the job evaluators had to tread carefully.

Toronto Maple Leaf hockey star Bill Barilko and Timmins dentist Albert Hudson both liked to fish. In April 1951 they were on their way back to the gold town from a fishing spot north of Fort George, Quebec.

Eglise St.Antoine
R.C.Church - Timmins,Ont.

Rev. C.E.Theriault, Pre.

*When hockey star 'Bashing' Bill Barilko
disappeared in 1951 the Leafs offered a
$10,000 reward for information.*
- City of Timmins

*The popular Porcupine priest has a Boule-
vard and Secondary school named for
him today.*
- Bill Boychuk

*Recovering a truck that fell down a surface
cave-in at the Hollinger Mine.*
- Timmins Museum

There were strong head winds which slowed Hudson's Fairchild plane, and the post manager at Rupert's House tried to persuade them to stay overnight until the weather improved. The two men pushed on instead and the plane never arrived at South Porcupine. The RCAF combed the area for weeks, but no evidence of the pair or their aircraft turned up. The Maple Leafs offered $10,000 reward for the location of their star player, but nothing came of it. Dr. Hudson had been a good woodsman. His friends felt that he could have made his way out from any crash site. Years passed and the episode remained alive, mainly when bush pilots yarned about the perils of flying in the North Country.

Jim Thompson came from the north of England to work at the Hollinger in 1953. He was not a miner but was trained along with several others from the old country. His annual wage was $2,500, at that time the price of a standard Chevrolet. As a miner he had an advantage over workers like Emmanuel Lalonde, a painter at the McIntyre who earned $100.83 every two weeks. Miners could double their pay with the production bonus.

Joe Hirshorn used Preston East Dome geologists and engineers when he staked out the Pronto Uranium Mine at Elliot Lake. (Since the Dome days, the names of all his mines had begun with the letter P.) Although government support helped, the Pamour directors considered closing the mine in 1953 to wait for better gold prices but kept on with the operation. The United Steel Workers went on strike at the Broulan Reef, and the mine, which had become a marginal operator, closed permanently. The Buffalo Ankerite was also finished.

Maggie Leclair continued to live in her cabin at Kamiskotia. Her second husband Billie died in 1954 and well-meaning people tried to get the 88-year-old woman to come and live in the Timmins Golden Manor, but she refused to move and stayed with her traps and fishing lines at her cabin at Kamiskotia. Alphonse Pare died in Montreal in 1955. He was a wealthy, respected man and his family all did well in the professions. His passing went unnoticed in the town he had named for his uncle Noah.

By 1955 the Porcupine camp had produced more than $1.21 billion worth of gold. Gold mines in Canada had shrunk from 140 in 1941 to only 60 in the mid-50s. Most depended on government assistance that paid from $2 to $5 an ounce. Since production costs varied from $20 to $45 an ounce, mines had to watch costs carefully to stay in the black. The Hollinger changed the skip cables on its concrete number 26 headframe. In four years they had raised 1,048,215 tons. The cables were an inch in diameter and 3,600 feet long.

A Steel Workers' strike over the winter of 1953-4 failed to close one of the mines. The Pamour had gone back to the Mine Mill union, so the south-end mine stayed open, along with the Dome, which had no union.

Father Charles Theriault died in 1956. He had been in the camp since the beginning and was often called "the Bishop's miner," as he staked the less fortunate to meals and accommodation. The priest's brother sang in the choir and could not tolerate long sermons. He would wind up an alarm clock which would ring if Father Theriault spoke for more than a few minutes. Maggie Leclair paid one of her infrequent visits to the gold camp when she was asked to demonstrate beaver skinning and stretching at the sportsman's show. The insensitive *Press* headline read: "Aging Squaw."

Leo Del Villano became mayor of Timmins in 1956 and served for 12 out of the next 20 years. He presided over a city where progress appeared at every turn. Conrad Lavigne had just gone from his radio station to opening the first television station in the northeast. The call sign seemed appropriate, as the letters CFCL could stand for "care for Conrad Lavigne." The new station owner helped to build the place himself.

Another entrepreneur, J.V. Bonhomme, offered new homes in his Melrose Heights subdivision and remarked when opening a new section that in the forties half the homes in Timmins had still relied upon outhouses. Bonhomme offered bungalows from $11,000 to $14,000 at five percent down. The advertisement declared the deal "better than paying rent." With the country coming out of an economic slowdown, new homes were seen as a good investment. The builder himself had come to the Porcupine years before because he felt gold was the basis for national economic stability.

J.P. Bartleman was a councillor in 1956 when he mounted a campaign for better highway signs to give directions to the city from Highway 11. He was unsuccessful and, in common with many northern centres, Timmins is still not well posted on the road any distance from the city.

The 300 Italian immigrants who arrived in 1956 rapidly assimilated into the community. In common with other recent newcomers, they began to fan out across the Porcupine.

In 1957 local fireman Murdo Martin was elected to Parliament. It was also the year that Fred Schumacher died. Fred Schumacher had been more of a speculator and financier than a mine owner. He came and left the area without much fanfare, and few people in Schumacher actually met him. A photograph of Fred Schumacher shows a grey-haired man with a warm smile. The Schumacher Public School has a portrait of Schumacher which was painted in the thirties and which shows his direct gaze. He is especially well remembered at the school because to this day his estate pays for Christmas gifts for the students.

A new outfit, Texas Gulf Sulphur Company, commenced operations in the mining field in 1957. The firm soon began to diversify and commenced an aerial survey of the Canadian Shield in a search for base metals.

A few of the close to 400 Hollinger Mine houses in the early fifties - Joe Rumelski

Hollinger directors, from left, Duncan McMartin, N.A. Timmins, Jr., Rt. Hon. C.D. Howe, Jules Timmins, A.A. McMartin, D.C. Finlay, J.A. McDougald, L.H. Timmins.
- Timmins Museum

As the fifties came to a close the Porcupine had a new airport and a social club, the Dante, which served not only the Italian population but also became a popular spot for Timmins dances and weddings. Old-timers heard talk there of the new jackleg drills, which weighed only 90 pounds and were so much easier to use underground than the bar-and-arm drills. There was also word of a report indicating that since 1943 no miner who had taken the aluminum prophylaxis had developed radiological silicosis.

Mining promoter Viola MacMillan acquired the Kamiskotia property from the Hollinger in 1959 and guided the copper-and-zinc operation to profitability. At that time no one had any idea there might be another base-metal property 14 miles away, but the Texas Gulf people were still looking.

An article about Reuben D'Aigle appeared in the *Toronto Star* in 1959. Then 85, D'Aigle was a tall, slim, erect man who remembered his early days in the Porcupine: "There was quartz all over the place, but no more gold in it than you would find in a marble quarry." Despite the poor showing, he had gone to Sudbury to register his claims. When the recorder said he would have to register in Haileybury, he let the matter drop. He even staked iron in Labrador, but at the time he could not interest southern investors. Reuben D'Aigle is still remembered as the man who walked over and just missed finding the Hollinger.

There were almost 6,000 men working in area mines in 1959 and times looked good, but in the mining game, lady luck often takes a hand.

Men punched the clock at McIntyre.   - PA 17583

95

Newspaperman Gordon Sinclair went underground at the Hollinger Mine in 1960. His last visit more than a quarter century before had so promoted the gold camps that unemployed workers flocked north seeking jobs. L-R: Glen Smith, Jim Prince, Sinclair, unknowns.
- John Kirwan, Timmins Museum

CHAPTER 11

A Fresh Chance

The Catholic Women's League held its annual Easter Parade, but generally people expected to see change in the Porcupine as the sixties began. The camp was 50 years old and its prosperity had fluctuated according to the viability of the gold mines which had created it. Anyone in the mining game knew that the days of the old mines were numbered. Hollinger president Jules Timmins helped pour gold bar number 18,490, which brought Hollinger production to over $500,000,000 to date, but old-timers recalled the adage that the day a mine opens is one day closer to when it closes.

On November 19, 1960, Hollinger miner Alan Rose had been on the job for just 12 months. Previously a plumber in Manchester, England, Rose had immigrated in search of a better life. His wife was to follow later. But a sudden fall of loose rock smashed the young couple's dreams. The novice miner was trapped underground for three days before he could be rescued. A big appeal in Timmins raised funds to enable Mrs. Rose to come over from England. Unfortunately, there was no happy ending. A month later Rose died from the injuries he had suffered in the accident. Tom Connors, not yet known as "Stomping Tom," was making his debut at the Maple Leaf Hotel at the time and wrote a ballad about the tragedy.

In late spring 1960 there was a bad flood on the Mattagami River plains. The Wicks mill's sawn lumber was scattered over 7 acres. The firm closed soon after. Porcupine people were used to floods, but this one was merely a dress rehearsal for a greater disaster. The Town Creek begins in the northeast part of the city and meanders through large culverts and open ditches to its outlet in the Mattagami River, not far from where the Mountjoy River joins the larger waterway. On August 31, 1961, 6.7 inches of rain fell in a stormy 12 hours. The sudden increase in water levels, coupled with blockage of the creek at some points, caused a flash flood. Roads collapsed, houses were flooded and some wound up at crazy angles. Many Timmins citizens were left homeless as a result. There have been many floods in the Porcupine's history, but this one added tragedy to property loss.

The Girard family lived in a basement apartment at the corner of Young Street and Wilson Avenue, not far from the Mattagami River. The couple had three children as well as a child that was a ward of the Children's Aid Society. When water surged into their home in the middle of the night, the father rescued the youngest, a baby, and took the child to his car. When he returned, he discovered that his wife and the other three children had drowned. The distraught man made for his car, only to find it under water and the baby drowned.

Fireman Bert Schaffer was working on flood relief and vows he will never again wear heavy boots in a similar situation. The police reported two unsuccessful robberies during the rescue activities. The Timmins Emergency Measures Organization came into its own in directing relief and clean-up operations.

In the wake of the Town Creek flood, extensive measures were taken to prevent the recurrence of such tragic loss of life. The creek was channelled and covered in several places. A year later the Mattagami Valley Conservation Authority was founded to control 34 square miles in the vicinity with a mandate to regulate flooding and provide more outdoor recreation. The Hollinger Mine was badly flooded and operations were slowed for several weeks after the event.

In 1961 the Porcupine General Hospital added 22 beds and the St. Mary's Hospital in Timmins completed its Pine Street wing, with 149 beds. The next year the fire department purchased an 85-foot aerial ladder. Mayor Leo Del Villano was in both national and international news when he suggested that trappers in the Porcupine could easily remedy the British Royal Brigade of Guards' shortage of bearskins. The mayor saw the offer as a good way to get publicity for Timmins. It worked, and the skins were soon shipped to London.

Wandering prospector Jimmy Jones popped up to make a statement that annoyed government firefighters. He said, "The best prospector now is a forest fire. The Department of Lands and Forests is always suspicious of us when a fire breaks out and sometimes they are right."

Jimmy Bartleman was 81 in 1962 but still found time to enter a marble championship, one of several events to celebrate the combined decathlons of Timmins and Matheson. At 81, he had lost none of his old combative nature and bombarded the Prime Minister and the Queen with telegrams urging that a former Timmins resident not be honoured.

Flooding in Timmins 1960.
- Mattagami Conservation Authority

The Mattagami River plain flooded 1960.
- Mattagami Conservation Authority

Roy Thomson was to be elevated to Lord of Fleet. Thomson had become a press baron and now resided in Britain. Bartleman called him money-hungry and an "alien." His arguments were in vain. Thomson was elevated to the peerage. Leo Del Villano had the last word. The mayor approached the multi-millionaire to do something to commemorate his time in Timmins. The man who made such statements as "For enough money I'd work in hell!" and "My favourite colour – gold!" was not interested.

The Coniaurus Mine closed and the Hollinger terminated its quarter-century-old medical plan, as the new Ontario Hospital Insurance Plan made it redundant. Jules Timmins retired, but Noah Jr. still represented the family on the board of directors. New techniques in mining saw the use of ammonium nitrate, a common fertilizer, used with a fuel oil to provide safer, cheaper blasting. The McIntyre found increasing copper reserves as its gold diminished, and it installed a 1,000-ton copper circuit in the mill. Soon that base metal exceeded gold in annual production.

Since the day in 1951 when Bill Barilko and Dr. Hudson disappeared, pilots had continued to keep their eyes peeled for any sign of their aircraft. The mystery was solved in May 1962, when a helicopter pilot flying north of Cochrane in the vicinity of Island Falls saw a pair of floats. A search party found the wreckage and remains of the occupants still in their seats. Investigators found insufficient evidence to determine the cause of the accident, but the mystery was laid to rest.

The Flying Fathers hockey team was formed in 1963 to raise money for charity. Comprised of Roman Catholic priests, the team travelled the continent entertaining sell-out crowds and bringing good will through sports. Timmins priest Father Les Costello had been a left winger with the Maple Leafs. "People never ask me for autographs after my sermons," he said, but after a hockey game it was a different matter.

Government assistance to gold mines was still in effect. The year 1963 was the first since the plan started that Pamour made a profit without government credits. The Pamour purchased the two Delnite shafts for hoisting in its Aunor Mine, as the Delnite was expected to run out of ore soon.

The Moneta Mine had been closed for many years, but it became news again when insurance agent Jim Thompson received a call from the owner of Timmins Coach Lines on November 12, 1963, telling him that five buses had dropped down a big hole. Timmins police officer Guy Piche first noticed the subsidence while on night patrol. Subsequent checking revealed that it was in an area where the mine had worked a glory hole, or open pit, from surface. There had been a raise angled into it from underground. The workings had been braced with steel and capped, but over the years, subsidence had occurred. The parked buses had fallen down the new hole. The pit was eventually filled and capped.

The insurance company paid up and no trace remains today of the hole and the buses it retained.

Back in 1959 Texas Gulf's aerial electromagnetic equipment had detected an anomaly in muskeg about 17 miles north of Timmins. They subsequently had found hundreds of similar readings in the Shield country, but five years passed before these could be investigated on the ground. In this new scientific way of prospecting, a magnetometer records the magnetic pull of the earth below. A transmitting coil projects the electromagnetic field into its ground and a receiving coil picks up secondary magnetic fields that are initiated in conducting bodies. On the ground, in 1963, Texas Gulf geologist Ken Darke found that the area was covered by several privately owned lots. These were optioned by the company and Darke drilled what became known as the Kidd Creek anomaly. The results of the first drill hole were extremely promising. To foil other interested mining firms, Darke moved the drill some distance from the anomaly and commenced a "decoy" drill. He was successful until Christmas. Rumours about a big strike had begun to spread by then. Over a 600-foot core, the assay was more than 1-percent copper, 8-percent zinc and almost 4 ounces of silver to the ton. Texas Gulf did not reveal this information. Its president merely stated in a year-end report that the firm was drilling in various locations.

George Bannerman died in 1964 at the age of 84. The prospector who claimed one of the first properties in the Porcupine never did get rich in mining. He stayed and spent much time in public service.

The Hollinger announced that it would close within four years. The story seemed the worst possible news for the city. The great mine was the largest single employer. But that bad news was almost forgotten due to the continuing story of work being done at Kidd Creek.

The American firm ceased drilling for the winter and was quietly tying up mineral rights to Kidd Township. Eventually Texas Gulf controlled 70 percent of the area. Rumours grew and in February 1964 Ned Bragagnolo, a Timmins real estate agent, spent $7,000 to hire claim-stakers to tie up choice sections of the Kidd Creek area. Within two months his ground was worth $2 million. On April 1 Richmond Grub-stake, headed by Pat Sheridan, moved 20 stakers into the area by heli-copter and staked 400 claims, as well as buying adjacent veteran's lots. Four days later there were 13 more crews in the vicinity claiming anything open for staking. On April 5 Texas Gulf moved four diamond drills onto its property. The rush was on.

On April 14 veteran prospector Don McKinnon checked out the names of the owners of veteran's lots in the land-title office at Cochrane. He found one lot equal to four claims adjacent to the Texas Gulf drill site. The lot was open due to non-payment of taxes. McKinnon raced back to the Porcupine for fear that another team was on the ground. He

Texas Gulf area stakers in July 1964, from left Don McKinnon, Ned Bragnola, John Larche and Fred Rousseau. - Bill Boychuk

One of the rescue teams taking a break before going underground to fight the 1965 McIntyre fire. The McCaa self-contained breathing apparatus stands behind them. - Real Seguin

snowmobiled as fast as he could, then snowshoed the last mile and a half. The prospector worked by flashlight from midnight until 4:30 AM. He was exhausted but had tied up the property. It became one of the choicest in the area. Such success was not a once-in-a-lifetime thing for McKinnon. With others, he later made a major discovery in the giant Hemlo camp north of Lake Superior.

By the day McKinnon staked his claims there had been 2,094 claims made in the Porcupine Mining Division, all in a couple of weeks, far more than had been filed the previous year. Meanwhile executives of Texas Gulf read in the Sunday papers of a "sensational copper discovery in Timmins." A call to the company's exploration manager confirmed good results, but people at the upper level stated later that they did not understand just how rich the find was and played it down in a press release of April 12. Four days later the air of caution was abandoned. A news conference confirmed an ore body 800 feet long, 300 feet wide and at least 800 feet deep. Initial reserves were of 25 million tons of ore under the overburden. This was a natural spot for an open-pit mine, and the silver would pay for mining costs. Texas Gulf had found the largest single base-metal mine in the world. The *Daily Press* headline read, "Strikes It Rich – Sugar Daddy Opens Vistas for Jubilant North."

The Porcupine experienced a mining rush such as it had not seen for many years. The two brokerage offices were swamped with 300 buy orders an hour, and those investors who could not get inside lined up on the sidewalk. Displays of rocks and mining equipment appeared in all the shop windows. The *Press* was full of the story for two weeks and revelled in such headlines as "Timmins a Healthy, Happy, Hopeful Spot." It was like the early days of the camp, when every second man on the street had some claims for sale, although not necessarily anywhere near the action. Old-time prospector Jimmy Jones even set up a tent under the railway overpass and started to sell claims, until police gently sent him on his way. The area was inundated with newsmen and camera crews from North American and overseas. These were heady times and more than one citizen noted that base-metal mines paid higher wages than gold.

As the flurry of activity began to settle, there were perhaps ten mining companies that had ground close enough to the Texas Gulf property to interest knowledgeable investors. Some people made money and a few lost their shirts. Viola MacMillan came on the scene after the main activity had died down. Every mining recorder and inspector comes across errors in staking claims. Some of these are not corrected and the ground becomes free. Four claims came available not far from the main strike and MacMillan used her appropriately named Windfall company to take them over. This ground also contained an anomaly, and Windfall drilled the site. There was no public announcement as to the values found and speculation took over. The penny stock soared, and Viola and

George MacMillan made a million dollars in a few days. Unfortunately Windfall did not see fit to report for some time that the drill hole contained nothing but worthless graphite.

Work began at once on making the big mine. A 13-mile hard surface road was built to the site by October 1964. The Ontario government authorized the ONR to construct a 16-mile spur line. There was no stable area of bedrock near the mine site, so the concentrate mill was built at Hoyle, 15 miles east of Timmins. They began stripping the estimated six million tons of overburden, which varied in depth from 5 to 50 feet. Some 7 million cubic yards of clay and muskeg were moved in that operation. The railway found its part reminiscent of the push north from Cochrane to Moosonee 40 years before, as the line was heavily backfilled all the way. Once the ground was clear, an open pit was commenced, covering an area of about 96 acres. Some area mines experienced huge labour losses as workers left for the high-paying construction jobs.

The Broulan Reef Mine closed in 1965, but out at Kidd Township the big mine had swarms of men and machinery on site. While daily blasts created the shape and initial roads of the open pit, a crusher was built to bring the ore to manageable size. A long enclosed conveyor angled up to large ore bins. From these the ore would drop into specially constructed cars, which would bring the rock to the mill at Hoyle. While construction continued, legal action was taking place. Texas Gulf was having problems with owners of some of the properties it optioned, and an Ontario Court of Appeal judge commenced the Windfall inquiry. His job was to look into the extraordinary performance of Windfall shares, which rose from 56 cents to $5.60 before falling back to 40 cents. The deliberations would drag out for several years.

Fire struck the McIntyre Mine on February 8, 1965. It was the first major fire since the great Hollinger disaster 37 years earlier. Miner Simond Floria, working at the 6,700-foot level, was the only casualty, but the fire was dubbed a mystery because it took a long time to find its location. The big burn closed both the Mac and the Hollinger, as both mines were joined underground. More than a thousand men were made idle because of it. Manager P.B. McCrodan would have 22 mine rescue crews from 12 Sudbury and Porcupine mines working on the fire before it was extinguished. They had to wear the new McCaa self-contained breathing apparatus due to the danger of carbon dioxide and carbon monoxide.

Réal Seguin worked on that fire. He recalls the greatest problem being in locating the fire, then being able to get to it. The fresh-air station was at the number 11 headframe and the men had to travel more than a mile vertically underground, then 3,000 feet horizontally to get to the fire area. This meant that there was not much air left in the breathing apparatus to enable the men to fight the fire.

Mine servicemen installing an air line to a surface stope at the Hollinger, 1961.

After three days, with both mines idle, 1,400 men were laid off and the economic effects were felt in the city. Between them, the two mines had 2,200 employees and were the city's largest employer. The firefighters battled heat and smoke in a huge area. It took a week to bring it under control and it was a month before the big clean-up could take place. The cost to the mine was huge, but lessons learned from previous fires and new technology in foam, fog spray and other chemicals aided in the successful conclusion of this fire.

The Paymaster Mine closed in 1966 and the Hollinger sold the water system to the city. Many of its houses were offered to tenants, who had the first option of purchase. There were 225 homes sold, covering a two-by-five-block area from Vimy north to Algonquin and Mountjoy west to Rea. Even after this big sale, there were still 83 homes in other locations which were sold over the next two years. The Ecstall Mining Company, a subsidiary of Texas Gulf, opened its Hoyle mill with an initial capacity of 9,000 tons of ore a day.

Noah Timmins' huge Tudor-style mansion in Montreal came on the auction block in 1968. Long passed from the family, its very size deterred buyers until an ingenious estate agent had the place cut in half and sold as two dwellings. Noah would have been saddened, since the Preston East Dome had already closed and the Hollinger had finally shut down. It would be hard to imagine the great mine, like a city underground, no longer leading gold mining in Canada. The mine brought out $556,200,241 in bullion before it closed. Typically, the company would survive in the other mines it owned and in a diversity of investments. Eventually it would wind up as a holding company under the direction of financier Conrad Black. As this mining era ended, the Dome celebrated the pouring of gold bar number 10,000. There was good news for the industry. Although the U.S. Treasury price for the precious metal was still pegged at $35, the world market price began to rise as it became determined by supply and demand.

The Pamour became the first mine in the Porcupine to use the new so-called LHD (load, haul and dump) equipment. Like the scoop tram, this method of conveying broken rock meant that tracked ore cars were no longer necessary and production could in many cases be increased. Over at Kidd Creek it was soon realized that the ore body was too big to be mined entirely by open pit, and work began on the sinking of a 3,100-foot shaft in 1969. This was also the year that court action as a result of the findings of the Windfall Commission was concluded. The MacMillans were acquitted of defrauding the public and fraudulently influencing the price of shares, but Viola was convicted of wash trading. This is the process of buying and selling stock simultaneously to give the appearance of activity. Despite the fact that the couple were said to have made $1,466,000 from the transaction, Viola was fined only $10,000 and

sentenced to nine months in a reformatory. Release came after seven weeks. Some thought Viola Macmillan was singled out and that others could have been charged as well. Many reflected that investing is a game where *caveat emptor*, let the buyer beware, always prevails. One aftermath of the affair was that many junior mining companies left the now tougher guidelines of the Toronto Stock Exchange and began to operate in Vancouver, where rules were less strict.

Texas Gulf itself was embroiled in litigation for several years after the mine commenced production. U.S. government regulators accused company officials of insider trading, but that was scotched when it was revealed that only one-tenth of one percent of all shares traded had been bought by Texas Gulf officials and this had been over a lengthy period of time. More serious was a case brought by old-time prospector Karl Springer via Leitch Gold Mines, in which it was alleged that an agreement with the plaintiff and Leitch gave Springer's firm rights to the Kidd Township ground. The specific property was found to be excluded from the agreement, so Texas Gulf won the case with costs. The son of an owner of one of the vet's lots brought action stating the property was worth more at the time of the agreement than he had received. The matter was settled out of court for $27 million, and with an additional $24 million paid to another option holder, Texas Gulf now owned the ground free and clear.

In the early seventies the Chamber of Commerce became interested in pollution, a topic which to that time had not been of major interest in the Porcupine. At the same time a survey in the clay belt area found that of 48 properties listed as farms, only 22 were rated as commercially viable. Even with modern agricultural techniques, the hard clay and short growing season once more confirmed the settlement errors of the twenties.

The Emergency Gold Measures Act was phased out after 23 years. The mines were making a profit unaided as gold prices climbed. The U.S. Congress raised the price of gold to $38, but strong private demand sent London prices to $65. The activity was enough to give the Hollinger a new lease on life as an open pit, and it was indicated that there were still reserves at depth which could be mined when the price was right. As of 1970 the McIntyre had extracted $360 million worth of gold. No wonder Sandy McIntyre regretted selling his share so cheaply. Pamour took over the Hallnor and Aunor mines and worked them for their last years.

Texas Gulf opened its underground operation in 1971. After the open pit had reached a depth of 700 feet, it was phased out in 1976. By the then the mine was sinking a second shaft to be ready for the eighties. The metallurgical site expanded over the years. At first the plant shipped zinc, copper and lead concentrates. In 1972 a zinc plant opened which produced refined zinc, cadmium and sulphuric acid. Two years later tin was recovered, the only source of that metal in Ontario.

Ed Hunt assisted Hollinger Chairman Jules Timmins to pour gold bar # 18,490 in 1960 but the mine's production years were drawing to a close.

- Timmins Museum

In the first half of the 1970s, the Canadian Development Corporation acquired a large holding in Texas Gulf's operation as part of the Liberal government's bid to encourage more Canadian-owned plants. The CDC made no attempt to interfere with the management of the firm. The people who worked for Texas Gulf had no complaints. In an unusual move for the mining industry, they received an annual salary plus bonus based on company performance, rather than individual bonuses, which can result in poor safety practices. With such incentives and good employee relations, there was no union in the organization and the 3,000 employees were happy with the arrangement.

Maggie Leclair died in 1972. She had resisted the romantics in the Porcupine who tried to paint her as "Princess" and had reached her century, spending her last years at Golden Manor, lamenting the loss of her cabin and traps. For the gold camp Maggie was a last link between the way of the wilderness native and the well-meaning white people. Hans Buttner outlived his spendthrift partner Sandy McIntyre by 30 years. He was careful with his share of the McIntyre pay-out and received more than is generally known. He went back to Germany, invested in property, travelled round the world, and even learned English at Oxford. He also took boxing lessons there, and later came back to Haileybury and settled accounts with certain people who had badgered him about his short stature and called him "the Dutchman" instead of acknowledging his German origin. He carved out a career for himself in industry in the United States. Later he returned to Canada to stake claims in the Porcupine, which the family still retains. He died in Kalamazoo, Michigan, at age 87. His son Fred reported that even at the last, Hans mentioned the Porcupine and the early days of mining.

The Porcupine had come through a roller coaster of rumours and mine closings. With the big new base-metals mine providing employment and the hint of new mines in the future, the economy was on a good footing. The camp was still vibrant and more change would come at the civic level.

The legendary Sandy McIntyre cut a dashing figure at fall fairs.
- Author collection

Noah Timmins shortly before his death.

105

The big Paymaster Mine in 1934.

CHAPTER 12

Amalgamation and Beyond

The Ontario government espoused regional government in the sixties and seventies. In 1972 Conservative minister Darcy McKeough proposed an act to incorporate the City of Timmins-Porcupine, and the new City of Timmins came into being on January 1, 1973. By that act the three municipalities of Mountjoy, Whitney and Tisdale, plus 31 previously incorporated townships, including Keyson, Connaught, Barber's Bay, Hoyle and Mattagami Heights joined with Timmins. Porcupine, South Porcupine and Schumacher kept their old names but were in effect suburbs of the new city. The combined land area came to 1,260 square miles, making Timmins the largest city in terms of land area in Canada and the second on the continent.

In 1974 the Mattagami Valley Conservation Authority became the Mattagami Region Conservation Authority and took in 4,246 square miles of watershed, including the Mattagami River and its tributaries, and part of the Frederick House River system, including Porcupine Lake and River. The Authority was now the largest in Ontario and the only one located entirely within the Arctic watershed. Another amenity became civic when the Timmins Golf Club was sold by the mine to its members at a nominal cost of $30,000. In honour of its creator, the place became the Hollinger Golf Club. The well-appointed course is adjacent to the town centre. The mine prudently specified that the property must be used for recreational purposes for the next 21 years. No one knew if the area underneath the greens would be mined again, and certain fenced-off areas still remind players of worked-out raises and former shafts.

Austin Airways was sold in 1974 to Stan Deluce, the former owner of White River Airways. The Austin company had provided bush-plane service to remote areas for many years. Jack Austin received the famed McKee trophy for his services to Canadian aviation. Timmins became Austin's main base and its aircraft operated on both sides of James Bay and Hudson Bay, carrying everything from food to fuel, even operating on occasion as an air ambulance service.

A Ministry of Labour report on silicosis research pointed out that no damage to lungs could be attributed to the treatment using aluminum powder. There were other factors in the prevention of lung disease. Annual chest x-rays, dust control, ventilation and general medical prog-

ress had all played a part. The fight against silicosis had been unquestioned for more than 40 years. Then the condition broke out among Elliot Lake miners. The Ham study of the problem concluded that regulations for dust management were not strict enough and would have to be revamped. Porcupine miners kept in touch with the situation through their union, but there were no cases of silicosis in Timmins.

The Langmuir nickel mine opened in Hoyle Township. Pamour welcomed back Roland Michener as a director after his stint as Governor General. A big secondary school would later be named for him. Pamour made a good deal when it bought the historic McIntyre Mine for $4.5 million. In 1974 its reserves were only two years of gold and three of copper. The veteran mine handsomely repaid its new owners with $3 million profit in its year of purchase and continued to operate for another 14 years.

The city hosted its first annual Ethnic Festival in 1974. The event, which continues to the present, included a parade and show to demonstrate culture and cuisine of the various national groups. Each booth represented a country of origin rather than one of its regions. Some onlookers noted that while the St. Andrew's Society was involved, there was no representation from the two founding nations of Canada.

Two years later all citizens welcomed back Timmins native Kathy Kreiner. At a reception in her honour at the Archie Dillon Sportsplex, the 18-year-old winner of the 1976 Olympic giant slalom stated her creed, "When you start out to win, you expect to win."

Lord Thomson of Fleet, plain old Roy to many Timmins people, died in 1976 at the age of 82. His son Kenneth took over the family business after working through the ranks in various company enterprises. One of these was the *Daily Press*. After he left, the building which had once been an art deco showplace, began to deteriorate. Reporters still bashed away on their ancient typewriters, though, and a big story in August 1977 was the opening of the Chartrand fountain on the south bank of the Mattagami River. A local realty firm built the 47-foot structure on the base of the former Wicks sawmill. The fountain circulated 500 gallons of river water a minute. In later years the fountain fell into disrepair but was

*Leo del Villano, Timmins Mayor
at the time of amalgamation 1973.*
                              - City of Timmins

*J.V. Bonnehomme, Timmins home
builder.*   - E. Duciaume

*W. Spooner held many civic posts
and became head of the Ontario
Northland Transportation
Commission.*   - City of Timmins

rescued by the present owners, Timmins Truss (roof supports), and it is once more an attraction with a sign announcing the City of Timmins.

Gold started climbing from $220 to $524 an ounce in 1979 and hit $843 the following year. People saw the yellow metal as a hedge against inflation spurred by OPEC oil prices. Inevitably marginal properties became interesting, and 12 exploration companies began work in the Timmins area. Pamour took in gold from an open pit near the Aunor Mine and began working the old Porcupine Peninsula property off Night Hawk Lake. The Dome suffered its first strike since the mine opened in 1910. The two-week shutdown resulted in a handsome settlement for the workers and it was generally recognized that wage levels at the Dome had been below the industry average for some time.

Don McKinnon is a patient man. Since the Texas Gulf staking adventures he had worked as a prospector across Canada and kept his eye on property north of Lake Superior that today is known to the mining world as Hemlo. He waited for ground to come open and staked it with the aid of his sons in December 1979. John Larche, his former partner in Texas Gulf days, also staked ground in the area. The two parties joined forces and staked more claims. The patience and hard work of the Porcupine natives paid off and they earned much from the sale of their claims when the properties were developed. Once more the area brokerages hummed with activity.

In 1979 the use of aluminum powder against silicosis was strongly questioned by the unions. The mines liked the practice, for it meant less lost man hours. Union organizer Bob Miner collaborated with McMaster University in a paper critical of many aspects of Ontario mining and made a strong attack on the silicosis treatments, saying that the aluminum powder was indiscriminately sprayed in all change houses and yet had not been sufficiently tested on animals. In vain, researchers in the program pointed out that the level of aluminum dust used in Canada was only one-eighth that permissible in the United States. The Ministry of Labour ordered the treatments discontinued. Now there was no effective prevention of silicosis except dust control.

In 1980 the amalgamated City of Timmins had 44,760 residents. Primary industries were still the mainstay of the area. The days of the log drives and bush camps were over. Forestry workers commuted to the cutting operations. The mines remained the largest single operation, but more than half of all employment was found in business, trade and public service. The Dome celebrated its 70th year of production and prospered, with record earnings at a gold price of $721.82. The city introduced the 911 telephone service for police, fire and ambulance calls. The province set up an air ambulance service based at Timmins airport and the call sign for the aircraft was Band Aid One. Fluoridation of the water supply was a big political issue in the polls. Voters rejected the idea. The last Worker's

Co-op closed, but the Consumer's Co-op retained stores in Schumacher and South Porcupine. Somehow customers did not reconcile political issues with their groceries. A fine new area museum opened in South Porcupine and its staff was inundated with memorabilia of the early gold rush days and the great fire.

On April 12, 1981, the "Pav" was destroyed by fire. Boys who had been fishing in the Mattagami River lit a fire to get warm. Unfortunately they chose to have their fire right alongside the building wall. The wooden structure was a total loss and the fire marshall ruled the blaze accidental. The popular dance centre was never replaced and the lot is occupied today by a used-car lot.

Timmins became twinned with Naushima, a Japanese city of comparable size. Two years later that city built an elegant new council building in the shape of a temple. The roof was provided by Mitsubishi Metals, which had designed and engineered much of the Kidd Creek plant at Hoyle. With all its advancements, Timmins was still very much a city in the bush. Deer, caribou, moose and bear lived within its boundaries, with beaver as the biggest commercial fur-bearer. So it was that when Princess Margaret and her daughter came on a visit to see the big mine and metallurgical site operated at Kidd Creek and Hoyle, the royal visit generated great interest as recognition of the more sophisticated nature of the place that had evolved from a rough gold camp.

Some resource companies had consolidated. Malette Lumber, with the Waferboard Corporation, ran a large operation west on Highway 101, while McChesney Lumber, a subsidiary of E.B. Eddy Forest Products, worked on the banks of the Mattagami River. Both Abitibi Price and Ontario Paper cut pulpwood for paper products in the area. Mining was mainly concentrated in the properties taken over by Pamour, the Dome and Texas Gulf. The Dome expanded its mill to 3,000 tons and had a new concrete headframe. The variety of metals found in the Kidd Creek ore body did not include gold. That big property added a $300-million copper smelter and refinery to its highly automated complex, the first such smelter built in Canada in 50 years. In a complicated swap of holdings, the Canada Development Corporation wound up owning the Kidd Creek operation outright.

J.V. Bonhomme, the man who had built so many homes to accommodate a growing city, died in 1983. Over in South Porcupine, citizens were able to visit the museum and consult a coloured brochure, *Chefs-d'Oeuvre from F.W. Schumacher*. Schumacher had been president of the Columbus Museum of Art in 1904 and gave his complete personal collection to that museum in 1957. The old financier's art works went on tour. The paintings were both valuable and important and like his life, eclectic and far-ranging. He had chosen from both American and European schools, with choice works by Bruegel, Lely, Bainsborough, Turner, Whistler, Sargent and Monet.

By 1983 the Dome had recovered close to 11 million ounces of gold and 2 million ounces of silver. As an old mine celebrated, new ones began. A big gold mine was carved out of the bush 99 miles to the north at Detour Lake. Much of the expertise and work force came from Timmins, and the mine continued to fly employees to the site on a rotational basis once the place was in operation. Closer to home, Texas Gulf negotiated with the International Nickel Company to bring into operation the Owl Creek gold mine, an open-pit set-up. The existence of gold on the claims had been noted years before, but at the time the property was considered uneconomical to work.

Ken Thomson came back to Timmins to open the new *Daily Press* office. Both press room and editorial offices featured the latest technology in newspaper production. Just down the street the building which formerly housed the paper and radio station sat empty while architectural conservationists tried in vain to have it restored. In Toronto, at the Canadian Business Hall of Fame awards, Tom Timmins accepted posthumous recognition of his grandfather Noah's achievement in mining and other fields. He said his forebearer "was always clearly aware of the risk-reward equation that is so vital to our free economic system."

That system was evident in the city named for Noah Timmins, where Pamour was purchased by an Australian firm, Jimberlana. Falconbridge Limited purchased the Kidd Creek mine and refinery from the CDC for $615 million. The new owner found a bonus in the sale when it investigated the ground beneath its tailings pond, not far from the Owl Creek Mine. Winter drilling through the ice located another gold ore body, and in 1985 the company added the Hoyle Pond Mine to the mammoth operation.

In April 1986 an Imperial Oil rail tanker car spilled gas, which escaped containment dikes. Although much of the gas was located and mopped up, about 1,000 gallons leaked into the sewer system. Explosions and fires damaged seven homes and 2,000 people had to be evacuated from homes in a 15-block radius. City and volunteer firefighters and police were kept busy for a couple of days as fires were fought, sewer lines flushed and a clean-up operation mounted. About 700 homes had utilities shut off until the threat of further fire and explosion was reduced. The evacuated people were housed in the McIntyre Arena. The only casualties were from smoke inhalation. Imperial Oil dealt with more than 500 claims for damage and was hit with a $108,000 fine by the Department of the Environment. Four years later this amount was reduced on appeal to $4,000, but by then Imperial had paid out about a million dollars in costs and compensation.

An advertisement in the *Northern Miner* proclaimed "Moneta is Back" in 1986. The once well-known firm in the camp which took its name from the predominantly Italian district had turned up as an exploration company and was situated not far from its former mine. The district was alive with exploration work. Old properties like the Hunter, Verdon and Tisdale were looked over while new gold prospects like Bell Creek and St. Andrew Goldfields were catching the interest of investors. Pamour celebrated its half century. The big mine marked the celebrations by paying the total cost of moving Highway 101 so that it would make a wider loop around its property and the open pit could be enlarged. The mine had progressed under the Jimberlana ownership and would soon be part of Giant Yellowknife. Keeping up with modern trends, its machine shop and assay department all contracted work out to other mining companies. It was operating the open pit at the Hollinger site and still involved in exploration.

In 1987 Canada's first big gold mine, the Dome, joined up with Campbell Red Lake to form Placer Dome. Canamax Resources opened its Bell Creek Mine. The next year the "Big Mac" ceased underground mining, but new owner Giant Yellowknife continued to operate the McIntyre Mill. Another Giant company, ERG Resources, began to use slurry techniques to reclaim gold from the McIntyre tailings. Methods of gold milling had improved dramatically over 70 years, and the earlier processes had left much recoverable gold in their tailings. One estimate put the total amount of gold in tailings in the Timmins area at 200 million tons, so there was great opportunity in gold recovery using the right process.

Work done on flood control by the Mattagami Region Conservation Authority paid off during 1988-89, when higher snowfall and water levels produced no real flood damage. The Authority had rejuvenated Gillies Lake after years of tailings and other abuse, and had done much to develop other area lakes. It also sponsored the Mattagami River Canoe Race, a popular annual event.

By 1989 the Ministry of Natural Resources had built up a comprehensive index of abandoned mine sites. The district has many former properties which feature pits, trenches, adits (horizontal mine entrances) and shafts. Many represent exploration work or projects that never panned out. Any mining camp abounds in holes in the ground that had money poured into them but which never returned any of the investment. Some sites had been producing mines, abandoned according to the rules of the day. Now shafts had to be capped, excavations and poor ground fenced, and the public warned about possible danger.

While such necessary work was done, the business of exploration and mining continued in the Porcupine. Mineral recovery is not all precious and base metals. From Penhorwod Township near Foleyet, trailer loads of talc are brought to the Luzenac processing plant located on part of the former Hollinger property. Talc is much in demand in papermaking, paint, plastics and cosmetics.

Despite fluctuations in the economy, Timmins has entered the nineties with the same confidence shown by its people through the first 80 years. Mines open and close, but there are still ore bodies in the area and prospectors are out looking for them. The Timmins Economic Development Commission points to large reserves of nickel which hold the promise of long-term development. Eventually the problems of tailings recovery will be sorted out and a lucrative new industry will create employment, as is presently being done with the tailings in the Kirkland Lake area. The city has become a regional centre, and the big new district hospital will cater to patients from a wide area. Perhaps the biggest recent setback is one shared by many municipalities. Without any fanfare, the ONR removed its tracks from Timmins in 1990 and the hoot of the diesel horn vanished from the gold camp. The loss of railway passenger and freight transport is the result of government policy which will have to be overturned if the country is to prosper.

Prospector Don McKinnon has stated that the people of the North must band together to develop the region and make those in the South aware of the contribution made by Northern Ontario to the development and economy of Canada. There are other virtues possessed by northerners and by the people of the Porcupine in particular. They are hard-working, warm-hearted, generous people. Such qualities are never mined out.

These carpenters sat in a cold, precarious spot as they "topped off" the peak of the new Moneta Mine headframe.
- Author collection

The site of the Moneta is now covered with industrial plants.
- Author collection

The main office, mill and central shaft house at the Hollinger, 1936.

CHAPTER 13

Five Timmins' Businesses

In 1990 there were 340 businesses in Timmins with ten or more employees. With smaller firms added, there are at least 500 enterprises in the city.Five are highlighted here. Two are small businesses, three are large. All are related to primary resources of the area.

Yvon Jodouin operates Underground Treasures in the Palace Mall at 223 Third Avenue. At first glance the place looks like a gift shop specializing in jewellery. There are counters filled with rings, pendants, clocks, belt buckles and book ends. Then one notices that most of the items for sale are made from rocks and minerals. Yvon's specialty is gold. He worked for Giant Yellowknife at one time. All his precious metal is from a stope on the 1,200-foot level of the Pamour Mine.

When the goldworker selects the gold ore, often much of it is hidden within the rock itself. The mine knows how much gold he has because a specific gravity test is performed before the samples are purchased. In normal milling, such gold would be crushed and the natural shape of the deposit would never be seen. This is not placer gold, where nuggets are found in streams in their original form, but gold recovered from hard-rock mining, where the precious metal is embedded deep within the rock.

Yvon dons safety glasses and protective gloves, then works away at the quartz with tools and acids until the gold is free. Much of what is recovered is small in size and is used to make earrings, pendants, tie pins and rings. Occasionally a nugget of gold is located within the host rock. In such cases the work takes a long time. Yvon carefully picks away at the rock and later applies hydrochloric acid to break up the calcite and quartz. Lead and zinc are removed with nitric acid.

One result of this type of work was "Little Joe," a nugget weighing 3¼ troy ounces. This big piece of gold in its natural state is not like the polished items one expects in gold jewellery. Its edges seem to flow around its core and are curled and barbed, as if they had been recently poured rather than having cooled after volcanic activity thousands of years ago. There is not the brassy aspect normally present in commercial jewellery, for this is pure gold, except perhaps for traces of silver naturally found within it. It is a soft yellow in colour. Yvon has other nuggets. One is called the "Spur," a delicate strand of gold which juts out from a base

of quartz. As for Little Joe, the craftsman gives the impression he would like to hang on to it for a while.

Christof Weidner has his store in the Porcupine Mall, South Porcupine, across from Northern College. Christof is an Austrian-trained jeweller and was the first in the area to perfect the art of removing gold from the host rock which he obtains from Kidd Creek and Placer Dome. He uses similar techniques to those used by Yvon Jodouin, plus more recently developed methods. In addition to nuggets extracted to stand alone or be mounted, he displays gold in the host rock. He also has trays of gold ore specimens and small nuggets ready to mount on rings or other jewellery forms. He displays gold flakes in pendants, as well.

These two retail businesses offer visitors a unique opportunity to see natural gold both in and out of the rock, and the option to obtain samples in a variety of settings.

McChesney Lumber is the last remaining lumber firm operating on the Mattagami River in the centre of Timmins. It is located west of the Senator Hotel on Algonquin Boulevard, right on Fogg Street, left on Poplar Avenue, then along Gillies Street until the mill is in sight.

The Chamber of Commerce offers a tour of the mill in summer months. Tour visitors can follow the processing of a log through to the final product that is sold to lumber yards. The loader is a big Caterpillar tractor which effortlessly lifts bundles of logs in large circular grips. Behind the machine which feeds logs to the mill, dressed lumber comes out of the building on a conveyor. This time it is 4-by-4 spruce. The firm cuts only dimensional lumber here, from 2 inches up in size.

McChesney started in 1918 and has seen many changes in the lumber business. It's now fully automated. Logs are no longer driven along the river to the plant. There are no camps in the bush, just contract loggers who fell and bunch the timber, delimb it, slash it to standard lengths for hauling, and load trucks for the run to the mill. As in the mill, modern harvesting in the bush uses much machinery and is capital intensive.

McChesney Lumber has assigned timber limits under licence with the province. The Pineland Forest Management Area is the size of Prince

Edward Island. From it, McChesney and other companies annually harvest jack pine and spruce. Large wall maps in the office show five-year cutting plans and areas laid out for replanting. The Pineland Forest is along the Upper and Lower Spanish rivers. There are no small operators in this business. The logs are hauled anywhere from 34 to 205 miles and cost-saving methods of production are vital. The mill floor is laid out like an assembly line. The logs are debarked, with the chips shipped to a pulp mill. Logs are turned and the size of lumber they will produce is determined by an electronic scanner. A spline is cut in one side so that the wood can be held securely, then each side is cut and turned automatically. Cutting to size is the final step. Nothing is wasted.

Malette Incorporated is located on Highway 101 about 8 miles from the centre of Timmins. Gaston Malette, the president of the forest products firm which is the second largest employer in Timmins, is in the business of renewable resources. Malette cuts and seeds. His firm never cuts more than is planted in one year. In 1989 they planted 7.5 million new trees. The operation is charted by computer and planning is the key to this big plant, the most modern east of the Rockies.

The elegant office building on the right-hand side of Highway 101 is the head office of Malette. It houses administration for the company's other plants in Ontario and Quebec. Behind the office is the sawmill, and on the left of the highway are the waferboard and particleboard plants. The mill produces 96 million board feet of lumber a year. Chips from the operation go to the pulp mill in Smooth Rock Falls. Waferboard is used in exterior construction. Malette turns out 40 million square feet of it annually. Particleboard is used in interior work. Ninety million square feet comes off the line each year. This product is made from poplar and shavings that otherwise would be waste. Some particleboard is shipped to New Liskeard for painting or laminating. In addition to cutting 909 cubic yards of logs annually, the Malette forestry division also builds roads and prepares land for seeding.

Tour guides introduce visitors on the Chamber of Commerce tour to exotic machines like the computer-aided chipper-canters, plus edger and trimmer optimizers, but the item that steals visitors' attention is a $3.8-million crane called the Kranco 30. It handles the more than 90 fully loaded logging trucks which enter the yard daily, each carrying 30 tons of raw timber. The crane sits on a 1,200-foot-long rail track and is 360 feet wide and 120 feet high, with an operator in a small cabin at the top. The Kranco picks up a truckload of logs at a time. It then slides along its rails to take the load for piling or to production lines. In the old days the same load would have been pulled by 15 horses. Malette stays on top because it uses modern methods to harvest and manage its wood.

The Kidd Creek Mine is located on Highway 655 about 18 miles north of Timmins. Mined ore is transported on the company's own railway system to the metallurgical ("met") site at Hoyle, 16 miles east of downtown Timmins on Highway 101. The Chamber of Commerce offers a tour of the "met" site, but mine tours are not available to the public.

The open pit has been mined out and now the ore comes from underground. Adjacent to the number 1 shaft is a big hall where miners receive their assignments at wickets somewhat reminiscent of bank-tellers' stations. Miners don belts, coveralls, boots and safety glasses in the "dry," and lamps are picked up on the way to the "cage." There are signs giving the latest production figures, the price of metals mined, and output targets. Miners descend in a cage about the size of a residential garage while two 27-ton "skips," travelling at 3,250 feet a minute, hoist ore to surface. Any sense of claustrophobia disappears once the 17-percent declining ramp is reached after the ride in the cage. The ramp spirals underground from surface and is like a small-town road, except for the fact that it is cut through rock, and to one side there are ventilation, air and water pipes. Every 400 feet, there are levels – which can be tunnels of up to 17 feet wide and 10 feet high – where ore is either transported or obtained through drilling and blasting. The place is so big that men are moved in Ford tractors or Land Rovers, and there is fluorescent lighting for some distance out from each cage station. Fire doors block every entrance to workings and the driver simply pulls an overhead hose which opens the door. After the vehicle passes through, a similar device closes it again.

This mine has refuge stations with toilets and lunch areas complete with refrigerators at most levels. Once away from shaft areas, the headlights of the tractor lance through the levels and they are augmented by hard-hat lights. If the tractor meets a scoop tram, the big low-slung vehicle carrying supplies or ore, one vehicle backs into a lay-by to allow the other passage. Occasionally walls of concrete appear along the level. These are areas where a stope has been mined out.

At some locations a giant drill can be seen boring holes into the rock. In others, blasters load powder into long holes in preparation for an explosion to break the rock. The blasting agents, which look like long pink sausages, are shot down the holes by compressed air. Such holes can be up to 200 feet long, 5 inches in diameter, and may have taken 12 hours to drill. The mine will use 300 cases of powder in this blast to move 10,000 tons. On any one shift there may be 250 production miners, but few are seen in a trip through the mine, as the miners work in pairs, each set of partners widely separated from the next. In another work place, geologists examine an area of massive sulphides. Pyrites gleam in the rock walls and there is much zinc. This is part of the original anomaly which sparked the great staking rush more than a quarter century ago.

This is a base-metal mine, but silver tags along in the ore body. Output has gone down, but there is still a production of 4 million ounces of silver a year, the largest single source of the precious metal in Canada. In one area where ground is considered shaky, a miner operates a scoop tram by remote control. The big machine weighs 30 tons with its 8-ton-capacity bucket. It can run forward, scoop up broken rock, or muck, run back, and even manoeuvre around corners if necessary. Back in the lunch room, while waiting for a ride to surface, maintenance workers discuss the mineral indium, which the mine has now begun to extract. It is used in the manufacture of paint and rubber tires, among other things.

Up on surface, a special room housing electronic controls is the place where explosives are set off after shifts are over and men have left the rock face. Three switches are hit in the right sequence and 10,000 tons of rock hundreds of feet below are broken, ready for the next working day. The silver output goes to Noranda for processing and the copper, zinc, cadmium and other metals found in the ore body take a ride to the "met" site in the thirty 100-ton ore cars on the company rail line.

The Metallurgical Plant covers a large area, with the concentrator alone being the size of six football fields. No attempt is made here to explain the various processes used to extract the minerals, for they are complex and highly technical. After treatment the waste rock goes to tailings ponds in the form of a watery slurry. At the concentrator the rock is ground down to progressively smaller sizes and then treated with chemicals to release the silver, copper, zinc, cadmium and other minerals found within it. The required minerals then separate for processing. As one guide put it, "The green stuff goes to the smelter and the brown stuff goes to the zinc plant."

At the zinc plant the concentrates of that metal are processed in order to produce refined molten zinc, which is then cast into ingots of various sizes as required by the customer. The copper concentrate goes to the smelter, where it is treated to become copper cathodes, and then moves to the refinery and emerges from that area as 99-percent-pure copper. Along the way, waste heat from the different plants is used as supplementary heat and energy.

Canada is the world's largest producer of zinc. Among its uses are die casting and manufacture of brass and bronze. It takes an estimated 20 days from the time the ore is extracted as broken rock below ground to the finished product lines ready for shipment across the continent.

Both at the mine site and the "met" site, the staff turnover is low. Workers there like their jobs.

One of Kidd Mine's own rail fleet at work 1985.   - Frank Volhardt Jr.

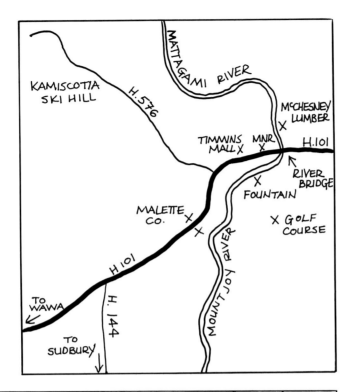

Tour West

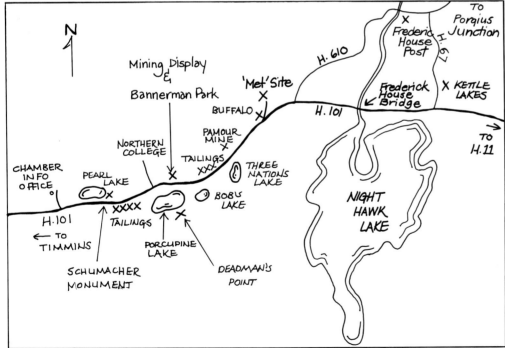

Tour East

CHAPTER 14

Touring the Porcupine

Business visitors tend to make their first stop at the Economic Development Commission, 273 Third Avenue. Non-business visitors may choose to start their tour of the Porcupine at the information bureau of the Chamber of Commerce.

The Chamber is situated on McIntyre Road in Schumacher. Turn off Highway 101 at the only set of lights in Schumacher. Signs indicate the way to both the Chamber information office and the McIntyre Arena. The Chamber office is hard to miss, for the great McIntyre Mine stands in the background.

The office is located in the former doctor's house of the McIntyre Mine. The handsome white building was renovated in 1990. Two rocks are located by the parking area. The small one is the "ripple" rock and visitors will soon notice the reason for the name. The other is a 15-ton chunk of ore from the Kidd Creek Mine which commemorates its founding. The rock carries a time capsule for the interest of future generations. The other outside attraction is a telephone booth in the shape of a headframe. A popular photographic subject, this structure must appear in photo albums around the world.

There is a mineral collection inside the information office. The staff have maps of Timmins and information on the various tours is available. In addition there are racks of brochures on both local and regional attractions. Posters on the bulletin boards indicate current events of interest. The summer is especially busy. There is a Mining and Exploration show in May. A Northern Graphics display is usually held in June. The month of July has Gold Fest, a collection of various events. The Porcupine Gold Rush Triathlon is held at the same time. This sports event includes running, cycling and canoeing, and is set up for both recreation and competition. The Mattagami Canoe Race is also held in July. Very popular Northern Ontario School of Gaelic Arts sessions are held at Northern College during summer months.

Across the street from the Chamber of Commerce is the McIntyre Arena. Barbara Ann Scott practised her championship-form skating here. This rink is the only local ice surface which is kept open during the summer months. Behind the arena is Pearl Lake. It is smaller now than when Sandy McIntyre and Hans Buttner first staked the big mine. This is due to dumping of mine rock many years ago. There is a small park with various items of mine equipment at the entrance to the McIntyre Mine. Imagine how Sandy McIntyre must have felt every time he visited the area and gazed upon the great structure that built on claims he practically gave away.

Visitors can wander in the area or follow one of four tour paths. One follows Highway 101 east, another follows the same road west. A third takes a loop around some old mines and winds up at the museum in South Porcupine. The city tour does not follow a suggested path but allows the visitor to select places of interest. There is plenty to see in Timmins-Porcupine.

Tour West

This tour starts from the Mattagami River bridge and follows Highway 101 as far as the Malette plant. The distance without side trips is about 7½ miles (12 km).

Prior to crossing the bridge there are two optional side trips. One is to the Spruce Needles Golf and Country Club. Turn left down Rea Street and go eight blocks to Wende Avenue. Turn right and cross the river, following the Dalton Road to the course. The club's world course rating sits at 71.2, offering a challenge to the average golfer. Retrace the route back to Algonquin Boulevard (Highway 101).

The second side trip leads to the big fountain. Turn left on Fogg Street for three blocks, turn right on Commercial Avenue, cross the river and follow Feldman Avenue to the fountain. It is adjacent to the Timmins Truss Shop, which makes roof supports. As you walk around the fountain, recall that this was the site of the former A.E. Wicks lumber mill. The foundations are still visible. Follow the same route back to the bridge.

When you cross the bridge you will notice to the left the large Canadian flag painted on a diving platform in the middle of the river. This structure was once a pier for the former river bridge. From the right side you can see the McChesney Lumber mill. Just to the right over the bridge is the Mountjoy Historical Conservation Area. The Conservation Authority created the park to commemorate the floods that took place here in years past. There are picnic sites and a children's playground.

Both natives and newcomers wait for a train. - OA 36371

Ojibway-cree logo

Further on, to the right of the road, you will see the district headquarters of the Ministry of Natural Resources, a wood-and-stone structure with flags flying from two poles in front. Pull in here and visit the reception area. They have maps, can point anglers and hunters to the right spots, and they offer pamphlets on wildlife and current programs. The rock wall facing the recreation counter is of interest because it uses area rock to represent the geology of an underground fault in the Porcupine camp.

North of the parking lot, you will see the tower for drying hoses used in forest-fire fighting. To the rear is a large steel building. This holds a library without any books. It is one of seven drill-core libraries located in Ontario. These core samples of rock are brought up by diamond drilling at potential mineral sites. The rock cylinders can be from one to several inches thick. They indicate to geologists the composition of rock and minerals in an area. Since roughly $25 million is spent on drilling in the province each year, it is worth keeping the results for future reference. If there is someone available to give a tour, see the facility. There are 15-foot-high steel racks of cores taken from the Abitibi-Greenbelt formation, and an examination room where an exploration geologist may be found splitting ore and studying the samples for promising minerals.

Return to Highway 101. Just a short distance further on the right is Timmins Square, one of the largest malls in Northern Ontario. Soon the road leaves the commercial strip and runs through small farms and thick green mixed bush.

On the right, at Highway 576, an optional side trip may be taken to the Kamiskotia district, former home of pioneer "Princess" Maggie, and the Jamieson and Kamiskotia mines. The area's ski resort can be found here, too, some 12½ miles (20 km) from city centre. It is a modern operation which in season has a 3-to-5-foot snow base and its own snow-making equipment. The hill has a 350-foot vertical drop. The adjacent Kamiskotia and Jamieson mines have been closed for several years, but their mine tailings offer a special challenge to scientists employed by the province. The mines were abandoned before regulations were made regarding reclamation. The tailings, or "slimes" in northern parlance, are deposited on the ground in the shape of a pond. Their contents are sulphite-rich, laced with copper, zinc and arsenic. Researchers are investigating ways of enabling vegetation to grow over and cover the area to make it safe and attractive for future generations.

Return to Highway 101 and continue a short distance to the Malette plant. The operation can only be toured by arrangement with the Chamber of Commerce, but it is worthwhile stopping to note the elegant wood office building on the right and the giant crane beyond. Park on the left-hand side of the road and watch this unusual piece of machinery go about its job of transporting 30 tons of tree-length timber.

Visitors now have the option of returning to Timmins or continuing on to Sudbury, Wawa or Sault Ste. Marie.

Tour East

This tour runs east on Highway 101 to the Frederick House bridge, with an optional side trip to Kettle Lakes Provincial Park, Barber's Bay and the site of the Frederick House Post massacre. The distance to the bridge is 16 miles (26 km).

Leave the Chamber information office and turn left onto Highway 101. An optional side trip is to explore Schumacher. Most of the homes are south of the road, and this is the place where most of the miners who worked at the McIntyre Mine lived. If you pass Schumacher Public School, recall the benevolence of Fred Schumacher. His estate still provides Christmas gifts for students and also awards scholarships.

Just about a block down 101 on the left is a small parkette. A monument in the shape of a stylized headframe honours Mr. Schumacher. Visitors often photograph the concrete structure, attempting to line it up with the real thing, a headframe at the McIntyre Mine across Pearl Lake in the background.

Continue on the highway and cross what was once a railway overpass. The lines are now taken up, but the former roadbed is outlined in crushed black rock. On the left the Carium Road leads to the former Coniaurum Mine. A little further on the left as the road widens you will see a gracious home set back among the trees. This is the official residence of the Anglican Bishop of Moosonee, one of the largest diocese in Canada. Area mines donated the land and material for the house many years ago, and it is appropriately named Bishopstope. The diocesan crest features an island, a passing canoe and the setting sun behind.

The stretch of highway leading to South Porcupine is practically straight and has two views of interest. On the left, see the Tisdale cemetery. Much of South Porcupine is located in the Township of Tisdale, and many pioneers are buried at the east end of the cemetery. To the right, notice a great grass-covered mound which parallels the highway for some distance. This is man-made and consists of tailings from the Dome mine. The compacted slurry is neatly covered by coarse grass and holds a fortune. These tailings were deposited when gold recovery was much less efficient than it is today. As a result the mound and others like it in the Porcupine will be mined one day for the remaining gold contained within them.

The highway curves at the Bruce Street entrance to South Porcupine. Since the community is covered in another tour, the visitor should stay on Highway 101. Pass the OPP district headquarters. The superintendent commands not only highway patrol and investigative officers, but also a northern flying patrol that runs way up to the tip of James Bay to police remote native communities.

Toronto Board of Trade monument to the fire victims at Deadman's Point.
- Author collection

The grave of Big Bob Weiss at Deadman's Point.
- Author collection

Continue through the traffic lights and soon the built-up area gives way to an open section. On the left is the Porcupine Mall. To the right side is the main campus of Northern College, one of several colleges of applied arts and technology in Ontario. Turn in here and see the historical plaque relating to the great fire of 1911, then continue round to the right of the main building and go directly to the west wall. Set into the building are two large sculptures honouring workers in the fishing and lumber industry. These were once part of a group of six panels from the old *Globe and Mail* building in Toronto. Former owner William Wright made his fortune from mining and his estate left them to the college when the newspaper building was demolished. Two more of the sculpture panels are at the Kirkland Lake campus and the remaining two are on view at the Haileybury School of Mines. In addition to courses offered by similar institutions around the province, Northern College has such trades as diamond drilling, forestry filing and mine engineering technician.

Go further east on Highway 101. The road crosses a causeway where the Porcupine River enters the lake. On the left side is a large display of mining artifacts, including the former mining recorder's vault. On the opposite side of the road is Bannerman Park, which honours one of the first prospectors and pioneers in the area. This is a good place to look back across Porcupine Lake. The houses over the water in the foreground are in the area that was once known as Pottsville. The middle and far end of the lake are where people stood in water up to their necks as they sheltered from the great fire of 1911. In the middle distance you can see the headframe of the Dome Mine, while the Hollinger sits back on the skyline.

An optional side trip leads to Deadman's Point. Take the first road on the right and follow the road around the lake. Close to the water's edge is a small mine sheathed in blue steel. This is the Hunter Mine, which has drifts running under the water. The property once produced gold and will again when the price of the precious metal rises enough to recover plant costs.

The cemetery is just a short distance further on. Many of the original graves relating to the fire are gone, but there is still the memorial cairn acknowledging the contribution of the Toronto Board of Trade to fire relief. A large slab covers the grave of Big Bob Weiss and his family, victims of the fire at the West Dome Mine. There is a pleasant view across the lake from the cemetery. It is hard to imagine the scene of terror and tragedy that took place across the water as victims helplessly battled the killer fire. Sometimes the yellow Ministry of Natural Resources aircraft may be seen landing on and taking off from the water at their South Porcupine base. Retrace the route to the main highway.

Highway 101 runs up a slight incline through Porcupine. This was once Golden City, the first settlement in the gold camp and the place where many fire refugees fled to safety. The road passes Bob's Lake and then Three Nations Lake, both formerly on the prospectors' route to the Porcupine. On the left there is another long tailings mound and then the Pamour Mine. The mine is not open to visitors, but just past its townsite is a huge open pit where gold is mined, and on the right, rocky mounds indicate where a decline ramp allows Pamour miners to drive underground. This area is closed to visitors, but occasionally one sees miners driving equipment across the highway, the lights flashing from their helmets, indicating they have just come up from underground.

A short distance along the highway on the left is the site of the Kidd property at Hoyle. The place is easily recognizable, as most of the buildings are green in colour. The plant is not open to the public except for scheduled tours. This is where both precious- and base-metal ores are separated from the host rock and then processed to provide the metals required by industry.

Some residents of the metallurgical site are quite used to the casual visitor. The big beasts which often crowd right up to the fence are buffalo. The Kidd management has kept a herd there since 1974. These buffalo are living proof that the plants, water and grass are safe.

A short distance down the highway, the Frederick House bridge marks the end of the east tour. An historical plaque honours Edward Orr Taylor's work in 1905 as the first prospector to stake claims in the Porcupine. Many prospectors passed this point on their way down the river to hunt for gold. Visitors now have the choice of returning to Timmins, driving south, or making an optional side trip to Kettle Lakes Provincial Park and Barber's Bay.

For this option, cross the bridge and continue on the Highway 67. Turn left at the intersection. The park is on the right-hand side of the road. Here, only 30 minutes drive from the centre of Timmins, is the only provincial park located wholly within a city limits. The park has 22 lakes and is popular for fishing, camping, canoeing and swimming. The unusual name for the park comes from the kettle-formation lakes. These were formed when the glaciers passed through the area and left huge chunks of ice. The glaciers gouged depressions in sand and the ice eventually melted to form the lakes. The waters are very clear, even though they have no outlets.

Resume the trip north on Highway 67 until it meets Highway 610. Turn left and follow the road as it briefly parallels the Barber's Bay portion of Frederick House Lake, passing Connaught before making its way back to Highway 101 at Hoyle. The main feature of interest near Connaught is the historical plaque on the left side of the road which recalls the Frederick House Post of 1784 and the subsequent massacre there. On reaching Highway 101, the visitor may return to Timmins or turn east on the highway towards Matheson.

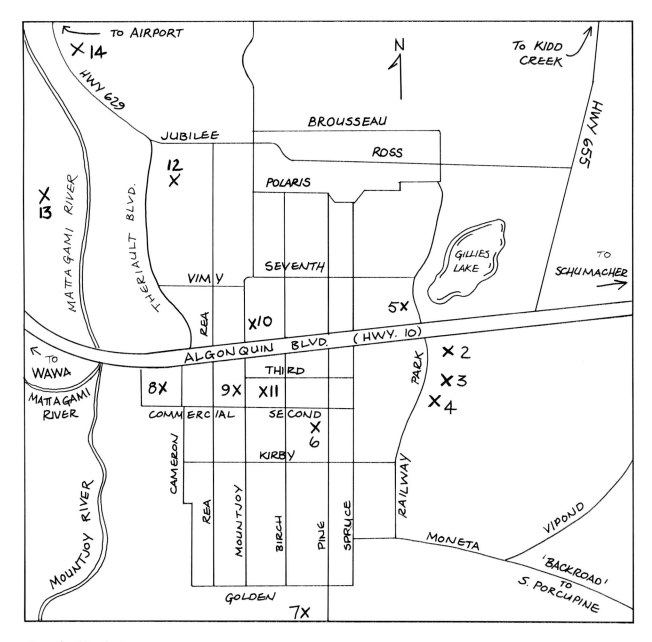

Tour the City Centre

Tour the City Centre

The centre core of the city has 12 parking lots where visitors may leave their cars while they visit places of interest indicated on the map and in the descriptions that follow.

1. Gillies Lake

For many years Gillies Lake suffered from rock and tailings dumping. Now the Mattagami Conservation Authority has rejuvenated the waters. The lake is stocked with fish and there are change houses, a swim beach, a picnic area and a jogging trail.

2. Hollinger Park

The park sits on what was once Miller Lake (before it was filled with mine debris). The 18-acre site has a children's playground, ball fields, a running track and a grandstand.

3. The Hollinger Mine

The property is accessed off Water Tower Street. The big concrete head-frame now houses a commercial business. The domed building close by once held 10,000 tons of gold ore while it awaited milling. The buildings just behind the Hollinger make up the talc plant.

4. The Hollinger Golf Club

Turn off from Park Street. This well-kept club has a few features not normally associated with a golf course. Rocky outcrops jut out between the greens. High galvanized fencing which encloses irregularly shaped areas is now mostly hidden by trees and shrubs. Golfers do not enter these areas in pursuit of lost balls. These spots were once raises to surface, former shafts or glory holes. The course has a pro shop, clubhouse and restaurant. Old photographs in the clubhouse show how the area around the course appeared when the mine was in operation.

5. St. Matthew's Cathedral

The church is at the corner of Hemlock Street and Fifth Avenue. This is the site of the building that was given to the Anglican Church by the Hollinger Mine. It has interesting stained glass and a tapestry commemorating Bishop Rennison.

6. The former Thomson Building

The building that once housed Roy Thomson's radio station and newspaper is at the corner of Cedar Street and Second Avenue. Closed, awaiting possible restoration, it is built in the art deco style, with many curves and flowing lines.

7. The Timmins Cemetery

The cemetery south on Pine Street contains a monument to miners killed in the 1928 Hollinger underground fire. It is located on a line at right angles to the service building on the right-hand side of the road. There are several interesting mausoleums. A fine white one with pillars is the resting place of former town builder Leo Mascioli. Another has turrets. Across the street is a small Croatian cemetery, well marked by a large white cross in its centre.

8. Flood Memorial

There is an empty lot where Young Street and Wilson Avenue intersect. A simple plaque recalls the family that died here in the Town Creek flood. Look around and see where the creek has been covered over as it runs south to the Mattagami River.

9. Ukrainian Museum

The museum is on Mountjoy Street South, not far from the Senator Hotel. Summer hours are from 9-5 PM Tuesday to Friday, and 1-4:30 Saturdays and Sundays. From Labour Day to the end of May the museum opens only on Saturday and Sunday from 1-4:30 PM.

Before entering, spend some time in the adjacent Kozar Park. The park features some mining artifacts and a statue donated by the Ukrainian Society in the USSR of the famous Ukrainian poet Tara Scheveko. The present museum building was built in 1922 as the Ukrainian Labour Temple and was the first ethnic and cultural centre in Timmins. It is still the gathering place for area Ukrainian people. There are displays highlighting the contributions made by Ukrainian people to Timmins in the areas of labour and culture. On what was once the stage there is a display of 750 antique and modern dolls.

10. La Ronde

The French cultural centre is on Mountjoy Street North, just up from Algonquin Boulevard. The attractive building does not hint of its past. It was built in 1922 as the Holy Family School. Francophones purchased the old structure in 1977 from the Separate School Board and renovated the place. Today it is a centre for arts and crafts. There is a lounge and meeting rooms. The public is welcomed to La Galeruche, an art gallery and gift shop. La Chaumière is a restaurant featuring French cuisine.

11. The Ojibway-Cree Cultural Centre

The centre is located on Elm Street between Second and Third avenues. The native people expect to have a new building in the future, but for now it is situated in a large house. The cultural concerns of the Nishsnawbe-Aski nation's 44 communities, of which 30 are accessible only by air, are represented here. Their logo features a beaver, fish and goose, representing the survival of land, water and air. The circle enclosing them is the sacred circle of life.

The centre translates and publishes writing in native languages. Native lore and customs are researched and recorded. There is an extensive media library. Books are produced for children using a curriculum which teaches their culture and values. An ambitious television program is produced for schools. One highlight of the year takes place when the

Retired miners who guide visitors underground on the mine tour.
— City of Timmins

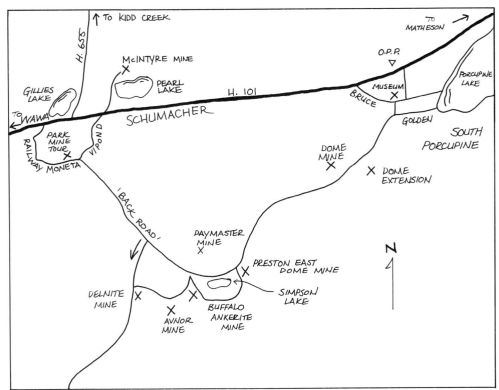

Tour the Back Roads

Logo of the gold tour: permission given

centre gets elders together to record stories and legends from the past in "Gatherings."

12. Archie Dillon Sportsplex
The sportsplex is located on Theriault Boulevard. There is a 121-foot (37 m) six-lane indoor pool with a separate diving area. Other amenities include a whirlpool and sauna.

13. Cedar Meadows
To reach Cedar Meadows, cross the Mattagami River bridge and take Norman Street on the right-hand side. The layout of this large equestrian centre is enclosed by neat white fences. There is a large barn, paddock, stables and restaurant. To the right of the entrance is a petting zoo. There are ponies, miniature horses and all standard breeds, including the big European workhorses. The indoor arena is used for teaching equestrian skills and the outside ring functions for "Western Days" and other shows. There are summer hay-rides and in winter large sleighs give trips through the snow. Cedar Meadows has riding buggies from an earlier age and provides white wedding coaches made by Mennonite craftsmen using traditional methods.

14. The Airport
Follow Theriault Boulevard and Highway 629 to the Timmins airport. This is a pleasant drive through an area where the city has expanded in recent years. For much of the way the road follows the Mattagami River, and there are some attractive homes along the edge of the water. The airport is the fourth busiest in the province. There are 11 flights daily to Toronto. In addition to scheduled airliners of all sizes, there are helicopters and bush planes. Next to the Kidd Hangar is the Ministry of Natural Resources (MNR) building. Ministry aircraft and water bombers are serviced there. Band Aid One, the provincial air ambulance plane, often sits on the tarmac ready for emergency calls. The big Canadair CL-215 water bomber uses the airport as a land base in summer months. Above the MNR hangar is the northern fire-control centre. This is a busy place in summer, as controllers direct aircraft that protect a vast section of the province's forests. One small plane which operates under the control of the centre is Bird Dog One. The plane acts as a policeman in the sky. When water bombers are working, it watches for other aircraft and warns them to keep away.

Tour the Back Road and Mines
This tour, which visits the underground mine tour location, various old mines and concludes at the museum in South Porcupine, is about 7½ miles (12 km) long, not counting side trips.

Go west on Highway 101 from the Chamber of Commerce information office. Turn left at the traffic lights by Feldman Lumber. This building was once part of the Hollinger Mine machine shops. The solid-brick structure close by formerly housed the main mine offices. Today it is occupied by various firms associated with mining. Turn back onto the highway and continue, turning left down Park Street with the Hollinger Mine buildings on your left. Follow the road around past the golf course until it becomes Railway Street. Near the Brewers' Retail store on the right was the place where five buses sank underground when an old Moneta Mine raise collapsed. To the left the J.M. Mill Company and Northern Allied Steel are located on the site of the Moneta district, where mainly Italian families lived years ago.

Turn left onto Moneta Avenue. The name changes after a while, becoming the Back Road to South Porcupine. On the left, opposite the ONR bus depot, is a small headframe at the entrance to the mine tour. There is a picturesque winding road, then the area opens into a big parking lot surrounded by rock and trees. This is part of the old Hollinger property. There are several pieces of mining equipment on display and the orientation building is shaped like the shaft house of a small mine. Enter the building and start one of the most interesting tour experiences in Northern Ontario.

Retired miners suit visitors up in overalls, hard hats, belts, hard-toed boots, lamps and power packs. There is a short talk and movie on Timmins and mining, then the group walks out over to the portal of the decline ramp. Mining in this area was not done by cage and shaft but through an inclined drift which could be reached by walking or driving. The drift is high and wide, so visitors do not get a feeling of claustrophobia. Along the way the miner-guides point out ore samples, methods of mining and the composition of the rock. Later there are demonstrations of jackleg and hammer drills, a mucking machine and slusher. They even have a way of setting off a simulated blast to give a safe but realistic impression of an explosion underground. Back on surface there are refreshments and free rock and diamond-drill core samples.

Turn onto the Back Road. Today there are houses set among the trees along the road. Years ago this was just a way to access some mines, and the only homes were clustered around each mine site. On the left you will see a road which leads back to Schumacher. This is the Vipond Road and it passes through the once busy mine properties of Vipond and Porcupine Crown.

About 1½ miles (2 km) further, you will see a road to the right leading to the former Aunor and Delnite mines. This is an optional side trip for those who like to view old mines. Most properties had a store, a school and residential area. There were bunkhouses for single men, miners' homes and homes for management people. Take time to look at the old mine buildings and the size of the installations necessary to win gold from deep underground. This is a pleasant short loop, but it is

Just above the Cedar Meadows Equestrian Centre, the Mattagami River cuts this scene from left to right and beyond is the area observed on the Airport Road.

- Barbara Dewar collection

The Preston East Dome in a new life as the 'Diep Daume' has a newly covered headframe. Currently the work there is custom milling.
- Author collection

The original two stamp mill from the Hollinger Mine.
- Timmins Museum

Tour visitors underground in the overalls and other gear provided. - City of Timmins

Original Hollinger engine at the outdoor display across the road from Bannerman Park, Porcupine. - Author collection

suggested that visitors return to the Back Road at this point because, although there is another route, it is not as easy to find.

Continue on the Back Road for about another 1¼ miles (2 km) and on the left you will see the big Paymaster Mine. This has been closed for many years, but now the Dome Mine is working to locate gold ore that was never recovered. Further on the left are areas where the topsoil has been stripped to the bare rock and some exploration trenches may be seen. On the right is the old Buffalo Ankerite Mine. It is possible to circle it. Visitors will find that, like most abandoned properties, it has an air of decay, yet not so long ago it was producing millions of dollars worth of gold.

Continue along the Back Road for almost 2 miles (3 km) on the right you will see the former Preston East Dome Mine that was not developed until many years after the great fire. The property is worth a look, for the headframe has been sheathed in blue steel and there is an attractive mine site. The mine is now called the Diepdaume. Across the mine tailings, behind the houses, is the road to the New York Porcupine Mine. In common with so many properties in mining camps, it poured more money into the ground that what was ever taken out.

The Back Road continues to the great Dome Mine on the left side. The big quartz knob where Harry Preston slipped and found gold like candle drippings is long gone. In recent years a big open pit has been used to recover gold near surface. On the right you will see the Dome Extension with its new concrete headframe. A residential area is now being removed and no doubt this area will be mined as well.

The Back Road comes to an end at South Porcupine. Go past Golden Avenue on the right. This appropriately named for the elusive metal that men sought when "South End" was the centre of the gold camp. This road leads to Porcupine Lake and curves up to Connaught Hill. A large grey block house in this neighbourhood was once the home of Charlie Lamothe, a well-known high-grader. Take Bruce Street and see the Timmins Museum and National Exhibition Centre on the left side. This well-planned and well-appointed building is one of only 23 such facilities in Canada.

The parking lot has an old ore car which has been sliced sideways to provide three seats. Visitors may want to sit and reflect on the thousands of dollars worth of gold and silver ore that the old rig once carried. The Outdoor Mining Court is cleverly set up to show visitors many of the machines and equipment used underground, including a small cage which was used to transport miners. There is also a skip which hauled broken rock and ore to surface. Children enjoy this display, as they can climb all over the unusual artifacts.

The museum has two galleries to display both travelling and locally mounted exhibitions. A highlight is the Costain Mineral Collection, and a small amphitheatre shows movies of the early days. One display is called

"Rainbow Chasers." The name is apt, for the prospectors sought their personal Eldorados and sadly few found gold. But many grew in strength and endurance. There are sections on the fur trade, including a simulated underground section and a trapper's cabin. The museum has a well-appointed gift shop which features books as well as northern and native crafts.

The tour is finished. Turn out of the parking lot, up Legion Drive, and return to Highway 101. Turn left for Timmins or right for Matheson.

There are lots of places to explore in the Porcupine camp. Many side roads in the neighbouring bush have abandoned mines and often evidence of new exploration, perhaps a working diamond drill. People of the area are friendly and welcome the chance to help visitors.

The Preston East Dome in a new life as the "Diep Daume" has a newly covered headframe. Currently the work there is custom milling.
- Author collection

One year after the gold was discovered, Porcupine had a main street with a fur dealer's store, Revillon Frères, the competition to the Hudson's Bay Company.

- PA 45326

Sights for Birders

Some time ago the Timmins Birders compiled a list of 248 birds that had been observed within the Regional City of Timmins during a calendar year. The list enables bird-watchers to compare their own sightings with those known to frequent the area. Those marked * are rare for the area.

Loons & Grebes
Red-throated Loon
Common Loon
Pied-billed Grebe
Horned Grebe*
Red-necked Grebe

Cormorants
American White Pelican*
Double-crested Cormorant

Herons
American Bittern
Great Blue Heron
Cattle Egret*
Black-crowned Night Heron*

Cuckoos
Black-billed Cuckoo
Yellow-billed Cuckoo*

Swans, Geese & Ducks
Tundra Swan
Mute Swan*
Greater White-fronted Goose*
Snow Goose
Brant
Canada Goose
Wood Duck
Green-winged Teal
American Black Duck
Mallard
Northern Pintail
Blue-winged Teal
Northern Shoveller
Gadwall
Eurasian Widgeon*
American Widgeon

Canvasback
Redhead
Ring-necked Duck
Greater Scaup
Lesser Scaup
Oldsquaw
Black Scoter
Surf Scoter
White-winged Scoter*
Common Goldeneye
Bufflehead
Hooded Merganser
Common Merganser
Red-breasted Merganser
Ruddy Duck

Grouse
Ring-necked Pheasant*
Spruce Grouse
Willow Ptarmigan
Ruffed Grouse
Sharp-railed Grouse

Rails & Cranes
Yellow Rail
Virginia Rail
Sora
American Coot
Sandhill Crane

Hawks, Eagles & Falcons
Turkey Vulture*
Osprey
Bald Eagle
Northern Harrier
Sharp-shinned Hawk
Cooper's Hawk

Northern Goshawk
Red-shouldered Hawk
Broad-winged Hawk
Red-tailed Hawk
Golden Eagle
American Kestrel
Merlin
Peregrine Falcon*

Owls
Eastern Screech Owl*
Great Horned Owl
Snowy Owl
Northern Hawk-Owl
Barred Owl
Great Grey Owl
Long-eared Owl
Short-eared Owl
Boreal Owl
Northern Saw-whet Owl

Shorebirds
Black-bellied Plover
Lesser Golden Plover
Semipalated Plover
Killdeer
American Avocet*
Greater Yellowlegs
Lesser Yellowlegs
Solitary Sandpiper
Spotted Sandpiper
Upland Sandpiper
Hudsonian Godwit
Marbled Godwit
Ruddy Turnstone
Sanderling
Semipalated Sandpiper

Least Sandpiper
White-rumped Sandpiper
Pecoral Sandpiper
Dunlin
Buff-breasted Sandpiper*
Short-billed Dowitcher
Common Snipe
American Woodcock
Wilson's Phalarope*
Red-necked Phalarope

Gulls & Terns
Common Black-headed Gull*
Bonaparte's Gull
Ring-billed Gull
Herring Gull
Glaucous Gull*
Great Black-backed Gull*
Common Tern
Black Tern

Pigeons & Doves
Rock Dove
Mourning Dove

Goatsuckers
Common Nighthawk
Whippoorwill*

Swifts
Chimney Swift

Hummingbirds
Ruby-throated Hummingbird

Kingfishers
Belted Kingfisher

Woodpeckers
Red-headed Woodpecker*
Yellow-bellied Sapsucker
Downy Woodpecker
Hairy Woodpecker
Three-toed Woodpecker
Black-backed Woodpecker
Northern Flicker
Pileated Woodpecker

Tyrant Flycatchers
Olive-sided Flycatcher
Eastern Wood Pewee
Yellow-bellied Flycatcher*
Alder Flycatcher
Least Flycatcher
Eastern Flycatcher
Great Crested Flycatcher
Eastern Kingbird

Wrens
House Wren
Winter Wren
Sedge Wren
Marsh Wren

Larks, Martins & Swallows
Horned Lark
Purple Martin*
Tree Swallow
Northern Rough-winged Swallow*
Bank Swallow
Cliff Swallow
Barn Swallow

Jays, Magpies & Crows
Grey Jay
Blue Jay
Black-billed Magpie*
American Crow
Common Raven

Titmice, Nuthatches & Creepers
Black-capped Chickadee
Boreal Chickadee
Red-breasted Nuthatch
White-breasted Nuthatch
Brown Creeper

Kinglets, Gnatcatchers, Thrushes & Mimids
Golden-crowned Kinglet
Ruby-crowned Kinglet
Eastern Bluebird
Veery
Grey-cheeked Thrush*
Swainson's Thrush
Wood Thrush

American Robin
Varied Thrush*
Grey Catbird
Northern Mockingbird
Brown Thrasher

Pipits, Waxwings, Shrikes & Starlings
Water Pipit
Bohemian Waxwing
Cedar Waxwing
Northern Shrike
Loggerhead Shrike*
European Starling

Vireos
Solitary Vireo
Philadelphia Vireo
Red-eyed Vireo

Wood Warblers
Tennessee Warbler
Orange-crowned Warbler
Nashville Warbler
Northern Parula
Yellow Warbler
Chestnut-sided Warbler
Magnolia Warbler
Cape May Warbler
Black-throated Blue Warbler
Yellow-rumped Warbler
Black-throated Green Warbler
Blackburnian Warbler
Pine Warbler
Palm Warbler
Bay-breasted Warbler
Blackpoll Warbler
Black-and-white Warbler
American Redstart
Ovenbird
Northern Waterthrush
Connecticut Warbler
Mourning Warbler
Common Yellowthroat
Wilson's Warbler
Canada Warbler

Tanagers
Scarlet Tanager

Grosbeaks, Buntings & Swallows
Northern Cardinal*
Rose-breasted Grosbeak
Indigo Bunting
Rufous-sided Towhee
American Tree Sparrow
Chipping Sparrow
Clay-coloured Sparrow
Vesper Sparrow
Lark Sparrow*
Lark Bunting*
Savannah Sparrow
Le Conte's Sparrow
Sharp-tailed Sparrow
Fox Sparrow

Song Sparrow
Lincoln's Sparrow
Swamp Sparrow
White-throated Sparrow
White-crowned Sparrow
House Sparrow*
Harris' Sparrow*

Meadowlarks, Blackbirds & Orioles
Bobolink
Eastern Meadowlark
Western Meadowlark
Red-winged Blackbird
Yellow-headed Blackbird*
Rusty Blackbird
Brewer's Blackbird
Common Grackle
Brown-headed Cowbird

Northern Oriole*

Finches
Pine Grosbeak
Purple Finch
House Finch*
Red Crossbill
White-winged Crossbill
Common Redpoll
Hoary Redpoll
Dark-eyed Junco
Lapland Longspur
Snow Bunting
Pine Siskin
American Goldfinch
Evening Grosbeak

Some came by jumper sleigh and others just walked across the ice looking for work in the gold camp. — Author collection

An Accounting of Riches

The gold and base metals produced in the Porcupine Camp come to a huge sum. The amounts that follow are from the earliest days up to 1987, the latest year that figures were compiled by the district's resident geologist.

Gold prices are quoted daily in the national newspapers. An interesting exercise is to total the ounces of gold produced and multiply that by the current value of the precious yellow metal. But place that final amount in perspective. There were many more operations which took investors' money and never produced a cent.

Mine Name	Township	Years of Production	Tons Milled	Ounces Produced	Grade
Ankerite	Deloro	1926-53, 78	4,993,929	957,292	0.19
Ankerite	Deloro	1926-35	317,769	61,039	0.19
Aquarius	Macklem	1984	32,000	7,200	0.225
Aunor	Deloro	1940-84	8,462,174	2,502,214	0.30
Banner	Whitney	1927-28, 33, 35	315	670	2.13
Bell Creek	Hoyle	1987-	55,180	9,558	2.235
Bonetal	Whitney	1941-51	352,254	51,510	0.15
Bonwhit	Whitney	1951-54	200,555	67,940	0.34
Broulan	Whitney	1939-53	1,146,059	243,757	0.21
Cincinnati	Deloro	1922-24	3,200	736	0.23
Concordia	Deloro	1935	230	16	0.07
Coniaurum/Carium	Tisdale	1913-18, 1928-61	4,464,006	1,109,574	0.25
Crown	Tisdale	1913-21	226,180	138,330	0.61
Davidson	Tisdale	1918-20	9,341	2,438	0.26
Delnite	Deloro	1937-64	3,847,364	920,404	0.20
(open pit)	Deloro	1987	49,567	3,134	0.77
DeSantis	Ogden	1933, 39-42, 61-84	196,928	35,842	0.18
Detour Lake	Sunday Lake	1983-	3,359,000	300,691	0.10
Dome	Tisdale	1910-	44,206,914	11,454,071	0.27
Faymar	Deloro	1940-42	119,181	21,251	0.18
Fuller	Tisdale	1940-44	44,028	6,566	0.15
Gillies Lake	Tisdale	1929-31, 35-37	54,502	15,278	0.28
Goldhawk	Cody	1947	636	53	0.08
(open pit)	Cody	1980	40,000	3,967	0.10
Halcrow-Swayze	Halcrow	1935	211	40	0.19
Hallnor	Whitney	1938-68, 81	4,226,419	1,645,892	0.39
Hollinger (Schumacher)	Tisdale	1915-18	112,124	27,182	0.24
Hollinger	Tisdale	1910-68	65,778,234	19,327,691	0.29

Hoyle	Whitney	1941-44, 46-49	725,494	71,843	0.10
Hoyle Pond	Hoyle	1985-	287,420	151,550	0.61
Hugh-Pam	Whitney	1926, 48-65	636,751	191,604	0.19
Jerome	Osway	1941-43, 56	335,060	56,893	0.17
Joburke	Keith	1973-75, 79-81	440,117	43,571	0.10
Kingbridge/Gomak	Chester	1935-36	1,387	98	0.07
McIntyre	Tisdale	1912-88	37,529,691	10,745,361	0.29
McLaren	Deloro	1933-37	876	201	0.23
Moneta	Tisdale	1938-43	314,829	149,250	0.47
Naybob	Ogden	1932-64	304,100	50,731	0.17
Owl Creek	Hoyle	1981-	1,358,812	169,960	0.12
Pamour (inc. Pit)	Whitney	1936-	31,807,685	3,235,833	0.11
Paymaster	Tisdale	1915-66	5,607,402	1,192,206	0.21
Porc. Lake/Hunter	Whitney	1937-40, 44	10,821	1,369	0.13
Porc. Peninsula	Cody	1924-27, 40, 47	9,968	27,354	0.27
Preston	Tisdale	1938-68	6,284,405	1,539,355	0.24
Preston (New York)	Tisdale	1933	2,800	153	0.05
Preston (Porc. Pet)	Deloro	1914-15	unknown	314	??
Preston (Por. Hill)	Deloro	1913-15	46	312	6.78
Reef	Whitney	1915-65	2,144,507	498,932	0.23
Tionaga/Smith-Thorne	Horwood	1938-39	6,653	2,299	0.35
Tisdale/Ankerite	Tisdale	1952	14,655	2,236	0.15
Vipond	Tisdale	1911-41	1,565,218	414,367	0.26

			Base Metals					
Mine	**Township**	**Dates**	**Ore Milled**	**% Cu**	**% Zn**	**% Ni**	**Ag**	**Au**
Alexo	Dundonald	1912-14, 43-44	51,529	0.07		3.93		
Can. Jamieson	Godfrey	1966-71	434,409	2.39	4.05			
Jameland	Jamieson	1969-72	461,805	0.99	0.88		3.5	0.05
Kamkotia	Robb	1943-44, 61-72	6,007,194	1.09	1.03	3.5	3.5	0.05
Kidd Creek	Kidd	1965-	76,700,000	1.99	7.54		144.0	
Langmuir	Langmuir	1973-77	997,903			1.5		
McIntyre	Tisdale	1963-81	10,162,640	0.62			0.09	0.023

Note: Cu (Copper), Zn (Zinc), Ni (Nickel), Ag (Silver), Au (Gold)

These dome drillers posed on their day off with the heavy machines.
     - John Kirwan, Timmins Museum

Nine of the 39 miners who died in the Hollinger fire were buried in a common grave at the Timmins cemetery.
     - Timmins Museum

Shaft sinking at the Dome Mine was a slow, dangerous job.

The Porcupine Song

Silver and gold in this country cold, are sought by each of us.
When old Larose once stubbed his toes, it made a lot of fuss.
But wait until next summer, when the sun begins to shine,
I'll show you a mine in dear old Porcupine,
Where gold is rich and fine, and I hope that I get mine.

Chorus:
> For I have warts on my fingers and corns on my toes,
> Claims up in Porcupine, Goodness only knows!
> So put on your snowshoes, and hit the trail with me
> To P-o-r-c-u-p-i-n-e! That's me!

Over the snow went "Right-of-Way" Joe, to see this find so grand.
The gold in the quartz was so big as warts on a schoolboy's hand.
Along with him went A.A. Cole, that four-eyed engineer.
Said Joe: "Now have no fear. We know the stuff is here.
To Cobalt we will steer, and we'll sing this song so queer."

Chorus

S.R. Heakes had heard for weeks about this Porcupine.
At last said he: "Let's go and see if it is just as fine
As what they say." So he took his way as far as Pearl Lake.
Said he: "This is no fake! I guess I'd better stake,
And then my claims I'll make another Kerr Lake!"

Chorus

Perhaps you think it's easy to get to Porcupine;
You hire a rig; you think you're big; you start out feeling fine.
When you get to Father Paradise's you eat some "pork and bean."
You don't feel very lean; you think you're nice and clean;
But you scratch and cuss, and it ain't the "pork and beans."

Chorus

Acknowledgements are due to writers Eddie Holland, Jack Leckie, Scotty Wilson, and their estates.

This was the most well-known stopping place for Porcupine bound travellers 1909-11. The shelter of "Lusitania" would have been sheer luxury compared to canoe transit.

Selected Bibliography

Barnes, M. *Jake Englehart.* Cobalt: Highway, 1974.
    Gold in the Porcupine. Cobalt: Highway, 1975.
    Cochrane – The Polar Bear Town. Cobalt: Highway, 1976.
    Link With a Lonely Land. Erin: The Boston Mills Press, 1985.
    Fortunes in the Ground. Erin: The Boston Mills Press, 1986.
    Killer in the Bush. Erin: The Boston Mills Press, 1987.
Braddon, R. *Roy Thomson of Fleet Street and How He Got There.* London: Collins, 1965.
Breithaupt, W.H. *The Railways of Ontario.* Toronto: Ontario Historical Society, 1929.
Epps, E., and M. Bray. *Vast and Magnificent Land.* Toronto: Lakehead and Laurentian Universities, 1984.
Gibson, T.W. *Mining in Ontario.* Toronto: King's Printer, 1937.
Girdwood, C., L. Jones, and G. Lonn. *The Big Dome.* Toronto: Cybergraphics, 1983.
Gough, G. *Gold Rush.* Toronto: Grolier, 1983.
Hoffman, A. *Free Gold.* New York: Associated Book Services, 1983.
Humphries, C.W. *Honest Enough to be Bold.* Toronto: University of Toronto Press, 1984.
Hyams, B. *Hirshorn – Medici From Brooklyn.* New York: Dutton, 1979.
Inis, H.A. *Settlement and the Mining Frontier.* Toronto: Macmillan, 1936.
LeBourdais, D.M. *Metals and Men.* Toronto: McClelland & Stewart, 1957.
Lonn, B. *About Men and Mines.* Toronto: Pitt, 1962.
    Builders of Fortunes. Toronto: Pitt, 1963.
    Canadian Profiles. Toronto, Pitt, 1965.
MacDougall, J. *Two Thousand Miles of Gold.* Toronto: McClelland and Stewart, 1946.
McElvoy, B. *Canada's Buried Treasure.* Toronto: McClelland and Stewart, 1969.
McRae, J. *Call Me Tomorrow.* Toronto: Ryerson Press, 1960.
Milberry, L. *Austin Airways.* Toronto: Canav, 1984.
Nellis, H.V. *The Politics of Development.* Toronto: Macmillan, 1974.
Oliver, P. *G.H. Ferguson: Ontario Tory.* Toronto: University of Toronto Press, 1977.
Pain, S. *The Way of North.* Toronto: Ryerson Press, 1964.
Pare, L. *The Seeds: The Life Story of a Matriarch.* Ste. Lucie des Laurentides: Les Entreprises de L'argent, 1984.

Patrick, K. *Perpetual Jeopardy –The Texas Gulf Sulphur Affair.* New York: Macmillan, 1972.
Peterson, O. *The Land of Moosonee.* Timmins: Diocese of Moosonee, 1974.
Phillips, L. *Noranda.* Toronto: Clarke Irwin, 1956.
Randles, A.C. *Geology of the Porcupine Range.* Toronto: University of Toronto Press, 1951.
Rasky, F. *Great Canadian Disasters.* Toronto: Longmans, 1961.
Roberts, W., ed. *Bob Miner and Union Organizing.* Hamilton: McMaster University Press, 1979.
Robinson, A. *Gold in Canada.* Ottawa: King's Printer, 1933.
Schull, J. *Ontario Since 1867.* Toronto: McClelland and Stewart, 1972.
Smith, L. *F.W. Schumacher: Portrait of a Renaissance Man.* Timmins: Self pub., 1981.
Smith, P. *Harvest from the Rock.* Toronto: Macmillan, 1986.
Solsky, M., and J. Smaller. *Mine Mill – History of the Mine, Mill and Smelter Workers' Union.* Ottawa: Steel Rail Pub., 1985.
Stortroen, M. *Emigrant in Porcupine.* Cobalt: Highway, 1977.
Stovel, J. *A Mining Trail.* Kingston: Queen's University Press, 1906.
Tennant, R.G. *Ontario's Government Railway.* Halifax: Tennant Pub., 1973.
Townsley, B.F. *The Mine Finders.* Toronto: Saturday Night Press, 1935.
Tucker, A. *Steam into Wilderness.* Toronto: Fitzhenry & Whiteside, 1978.
West, B. *The Fire Birds.* Toronto: Queen's Printer, 1974.

Pamphlets, Papers & Articles
Annual Reports. North Bay, T&NO Railway.
Annual Report Dept. Lands & Forests. Toronto: King's Printer, 1912.
An Archaeological Site Survey of Timmins District. Cochrane: Ministry of Natural Resources, 1974.
Brown, L. "The Golden Years." *Canadian Geographical Journal,* vol. 74, 1967.
Brown, L. *Golden Porcupine.* Toronto: Queen's Printer, 1974.
Mattagami Region Conservation Report. Toronto: MNR, 1979.
Canada Year Book. Ottawa: King's Printer, 1911.
Conservation of Life and Property from Fire. Toronto: Ontario Fire League, 1920.
Cole, A. "The Mining Industry in Relation to the T&NO." *The Canadian Mining Journal,* vol. 34:294, 1914.

Cole, A. *The Mining Industry in that part of Northern Ontario Serviced by the* T&NO. Toronto: King's Printer, 1911.

DiGiamaco, J. *They Live in the Moneta*. Downsview, Ontario: York University, 1982.

DiGiamaco, J. *The Italians of Timmins*. Downsview, Ontario: York University, 1982.

The Evening Telegram. Toronto, Aug. 1, 1911.

The Globe. Toronto, Aug. 1-5, 1911.

Gray, J. "The Fire that Wiped Out Porcupine." *Macleans*, Feb. 1984.

Knight, C.W. "Prospecting in Ontario." *Canadian Mining Journal*, vol. 71, 1951.

Kee, H. "Sinking Operations at McIntyre #11 Shaft." *Canadian Metallurgical Bulletin*, April 1926.

The Gold Community. Toronto: Timmins Industrial Commission, 1956.

Lam, D. "The Whites Accept Us Chinese Now." *The Changing Dynamics of Being Chinese in Timmins*. Downsview, Ontario: York University, 1983.

Land Use Guidelines – Timmins District. Toronto: MNR, 1983.

Leslie, A. *Large Forest Fires in Ontario*. Toronto: Dept. Lands & Forests, n.d.

Macbeth, R.G. "Empire of the North." T&NO pamphlet #10, Toronto, 1912.

"T&NO Extension and a Custom Smelter." *The Canadian Mining Journal*, 48:303-304, 1927.

The Ontario and Quebec Goldfields. Toronto: Legislative Library, 1911.

The Porcupine Advance, Timmins.

"The Porcupine Mining District," *The Canadian Mining Journal*. Porcupine series 2, 1911.

The Journal, Sudbury, July 13 and 10, 1911.

Report of the Royal Commission on Mineral Resources of Ontario. Toronto: Queen's Printer, 1981.

The Star. Toronto, Aug. 1, 1911.

The Story of The Prospector and The Porcupine 1909-1939. Timmins: Prospectors' Association, 1939.

Souvenir Booklet, The Silver Anniversary of Porcupine, Timmins, 1937.

Timmins Daily Press, Timmins.

Vasiliadis, P. *The Truth is Sometimes Very Dangerous – Ethnic Workers and the Rise and Fall of the Workers' Co-operative in the Porcupine Camp*, Downsview, Ontario: York University, 1983.

Whitson, J. *Fire Losses in Ontario*. Ottawa: Federal Commission, 1912.

Timmins with the McIntyre Mine in the foreground in this early thirties view.

- Author collection

These Finn miners smiled but their work was hard and dangerous, lit only by the candles on their hats. - Timmins Museum